for Angela and David Davies,

certainly not Cornish. but still great.

With love from

Crispin Gill

July 1995

The

T CORNISH FAMILIES

Y OF THE PEOPLE AND THEIR HOUSES

The
GREAT CORNISH FAMILIES
A HISTORY OF THE PEOPLE AND THEIR HOUSES

CRISPIN GILL

CORNWALL BOOKS

First published in 1995 by Cornwall Books

ISBN 1 871060 25 7

British Library Cataloguing-in-Publication Data
CIP data for this book is available from the British Library

CORNWALL BOOKS
Halsgrove House
Lower Moor Way
Tiverton EX16 6SS

Telephone: 01884 243242
Facsimile: 01884 243325

Printed in Great Britain by Longdunn Press Ltd., Bristol.

DEDICATION

To ALISON HODGE
who produced the idea for this book

and A.L. ROWSE
who suggested that I should write it

and my WIFE BETTY
who enoucouraged me in the writing

Contents

Introduction

Cornwall is rich in landed gentry but short on titled aristocrats. It is always believed that the existence of the Duke of Cornwall, the great inheritance that the eldest son of a sovereign assumes on birth, has always mitigated against the rise of an aristocracy, or any major landed family, in the county. So Cornwall has many comparatively small estates, but no families with vast holdings.

In Cornwall today there are only two earls, one viscount, one baron and five baronets. There is one extinct earldom, two baronies still surviving in families no longer linked with Cornwall, and a number of baronies which have died out. Of the twenty-two families treated in this book, only a dozen remain in the county.

The choice of families to be included had to be abitrary. There have been important families in past centuries who have vanished from the scene entirely. Some of these, like the Arundells and the Grenvilles, were so important that they could not be forgotten. There is the couplet of Civil War days:

> *The four wheels of Charles's Wain,*
> *Grenville, Godolphin, Trevanion, Slanning, slain.*

Not one of these families survive in Cornwall, any more than those in that other well-known quotation: 'A Godolphin was never known to want for wit: a Trelawny courage, or a Grenville loyalty'.

There have been other men who in their time made a great stir but founded no dynasty to continue their name.

Among them was William Lemon, a poor man's son who became the manager of the tin-smelting works at Chyandour and then married well in 1724. He invested his wife's money in developing Wheal Fortune, in Gwennap. This brought him a fortune of £10 000 and he expanded his influence through many of the surrounding mines, working them on an unprecedented scale. He built himself a splendid town house in Truro (the finest Georgian street in the city is still named Lemon Street). Lemon's architect then designed him a mansion at Carclew, on the edge of the Gwennap mining area. He died a baronet in 1760. His family lived at Carclew for another century but the last baronet died in 1864. The estate went to a Tremayne nephew but it burnt down in 1924, and now only the gardens survive.

Philip Hawkins bought Trewithen, near Probus, in 1715 out of the fortune his lawyer father made from mining disputes, and he and his successors developed a Georgian house and gardens of great elegance. Christopher, who succeeded in the late eighteenth century, vastly improved the family fortunes with mining investments and his unabashed borough-mongering. He bought, sold and swopped Parliamentary seats in west Cornwall with zeal and energy. He was made a baronet in 1799 but died a bachelor in 1829. The last Hawkins to live at Trewithen died in 1903; the estate passed to a nephew, George Johnstone, who made a great name for himself as a gardener and plantsman. From him the estate passed to a grandchild.

Sir Richard Tangye, the son of an Illogan miner, was a nineteenth-century engineer who set up business in Birmingham and with his brother founded Birmingham Art Gallery. He bought Glendurgal near Newquay as a summer house, now it is an hotel. The family is best known today for two writers, the late Nigel and Derek, author of the immensely popular *A Gull on the Roof* series.

The Harveys of Hayle are another major mercantile figures in the story of Cornish engineering and mining.

The Corytons of Pentillie are another family whose records go back over the centuries. In the time of King Charles I, William – 'Cornwall's late glory, now its grief' was his epitaph – worked with Eliot in opposition to the king. He it was who held the Speaker in his chair while

Pentillie, home of Corytons for centuries, sits high above the Tamar although trees now hide it from the river. A drawing of 1813.

Eliot made his great speech, and Coryton went to the Tower for his pains. But when it came to the crunch he could not oppose his king, and joined the Royalist ranks. It was his daughter Phillipa who went to a rabid Parliamentary preacher, Hugh Peters, in Plymouth in 1646 with overtures from her father, and led Peters through the warring lines to arrange the surrender of Mount

Sir Reginald Mohun, whose family owned Boconnoc for a spell in the seventeenth century, and whose daughter married the first Trelawny baronet.

Edgcumbe. William Coryton died in 1651, and the family has lived quietly on Tamarside ever since.

The name of Buller, of Shillingham and Morval, in east Cornwall, keeps cropping up. They owned several east Cornwall Parliamentary seats, and Charles Buller, a friend of Thackeray's, was the first MP for Liskeard after the Reform Bill. The family produced a judge in the previous century, and a general who distinguished himself in the Crimea, but they had little to do with Cornwall.

One could dilate on the Tremaynes of Heligan or the Carminows, the Roscarrocks; a whole range of names. There are families which had a name in Tudor times but are now of historical interest only. Great English families like the Bonvilles, de Veres, Warwicks and Spencers, above all the Courtenay Earls of Devon, held land in Cornwall but never resided.

One Courtenay early on held Inswork in East Cornwall and was created Lord Millbrook. Another married the last of the Carminows of Boconnoc. The estate passed to the Mohuns (another English family) and then to Thomas Pitt, a former governor of Madras who had amassed a hugh fortune and sold the famous Pitt Diamond to buy Boconnoc. His great-grandson was ennobled as the first Lord Camelford and played some part in developing china clay. His uncle was William Pitt, first Earl of Chatham, and his cousin William Pitt the Younger, the two great Prime Ministers. The second Lord Camelford was a commander in the navy from which he was twice sacked; he came home to lead a dissolute London life, was shot in a duel in 1804 and the title died with him.

Only half of the twenty-two families in this book are of Cornish origin, and not all of them are necessarily of Cornish stock. The nearer their origins are to the Tamar, the more likely they are to be Anglo-Saxon. Five of them claim Norman descent. The other quarter migrated into Cornwall from England. A large number owe their estates to fortunate marriages; some like the Prideaux and the Eliots to property buying at the Dissolution of the monasteries, one or two like the Robartes and the Rashleighs to their skills in Tudor trade, some to their success as lawyers, and a couple were eighteenth-century merchants in tin.

There has inevitably been some looking down of patrician noses at the Johnny-come-latelies. The ancient line of Vyvyan could say of the Vivians, who only became important when Hussey Vivian distinguished himself at Waterloo and bought Glynn, that 'the Vivians with an "I" would give their eyes to be Vyvyans with a "Y"'. But time conquers all; whether for love or for advantageous linking of estates, all the families are related by marriage. 'All Cornish gentlemen are cousins' is an old remark. In fact the Arundells made themselves unpopular in late medieval times by marrying so much out of Cornwall. The Grenvilles in particular were offended: they resented the idea that the local gentry were not good enough for the Arundells.

These, the greatest of all the Cornish families, have vanished from the county. The names are still to be found in the telephone directory but the main line has died and their great houses know them no more. On the title page of his novel, *The Blanket of the Dark*, John Buchan has a quotation from 1625. It can be rewritten for Cornwall.

> *Where is Basset? Where is Godolphin? Where is Grenville? Nay, which is more and most of all, where is Arundell? They are entombed in the urns and sepulchres of mortality.*

The chief mining district of Cornwall photographed in 1892 by J.C. Burrow, looking east from a Dolcoath engine house. Mining areas like this made the wealth of many of the great Cornish families.

The Great Arundells of Lanherne

One of the loveliest and least-known corners of Cornwall is the Vale of Lanherne, a wooded valley running down to the North Coast between Newquay and Padstow. Buried in the trees is the pleasant village of St Mawgan, its church full of memorials to the Arundell family. Opposite the church a high wall cuts off from public gaze a Carmelite nunnery, Lanherne.

For centuries this was the home of 'The Great Arundells', as they were known, the richest and most powerful family in the county. Originally they came over with the Conqueror. On their coat of arms are six swallows, from whose French name *hirondelle* they are said to take their name.

Lanherne was originally given to the butler of the wine cellar to King Henry II (1154-89). An Arundell already settled in St Ervan married the last heiress of the butler's family, moved to Lanherne in 1231, and for generation after generation the family, by rich marriages to heiresses, built up their power and wealth.

An early Arundell was Marshall of England. In 1260 Sir Ralph was sheriff of Cornwall. In 1379 Sir John was placed in command of a fleet by Richard II to aid the Duke of Brittany. The story goes that when fitting out the fleet he broke into a nunnery near Southampton and carried off several of the nuns. He was pursued by divine retribution in the shape of a fierce gale off the Irish coast. The nuns were thrown overboard to lighten the ship but to no avail; twenty-five ships were lost along with the wicked Sir John and most of the crews.

His grandson, Sir John the Magnificent (he owned fifty-two suits of cloth-of-gold!) was a naval commander, sheriff four times, and MP for the county in 1422-3. His son, another John, was the richest man in Cornwall with estates worth £2000 a year.

In the Wars of the Roses the family sided with the Lancastrians and John Arundell, Bishop of Chichester, was domestic chaplain and confessor to King Henry VI. He died in 1477, by which time another John Arundell was making his way in the church, becoming Bishop of Lichfield in 1496 and of Exeter in 1502. He died in 1504.

When Richard III usurped the throne in 1483 he outraged not just the Arundells and the other Lancastrian gentlemen of the West, but many Yorkists as well. Sir Thomas Arundell was among those supporting the proclamation of Henry Tudor, Earl of Richmond, the Lancastrian claimant to the throne. But this move failed, even though Richmond did come into Cawsand Bay in East Cornwall. Arundell, along with Edgcumbe and other Cornish gentlemen, fled to Brittany to join Richmond in exile. Not until after Henry Tudor's defeat of Richard III at Bosworth was Arundell able to return to Lanherne. His son John refused a peerage from Wolsey and, apart from attending the Field of the Cloth of Gold, was content to limit his interest to Cornish affairs.

1

Lanherne, home for centuries of the Arundells. It is now a nunnery, enclosed by a high wall.

But the split with Rome was both to sadden and diminish the Arundells. They were unhappy with the new religion, and Humphrey became the leader of the Cornish Rebellion of 1549 in protest against the new prayer book. He led the Cornish army to besiege Exeter, where the rebellion was crushed, and Humphrey was executed the following year. Not until Mary Tudor came to the throne did the Arundells win back favour, and under Elizabeth they continued to hold positions of trust in the county.

The Arundells gradually emerged as the leaders of the Catholics in Cornwall, and increasingly in trouble with authority. What is more, their wealth and their practice of marrying outside the county, as though the local heiresses were not good enough for them, made them more and more at odds with their neighbours, chiefly the Grenvilles of Stowe. When Richard Grenville became sheriff in 1576 he began a vendetta against his Catholic neighbours. He arrested a Catholic priest at the home of Francis Tregian – a nephew of Sir John Arundell. The priest, now the Blessed Cuthbert Mayne, was executed, and Tregian imprisoned. John Arundell was arrested for non-attendance at church on Sundays and was imprisoned for a time.

From now on he was constantly in trouble, and spent nine years in confinement at Ely Palace, Holborn. He had to pay heavy fines for his refusal to attend church. When he died in 1587 the power of the Cornish Arundells ended. The heavy fines crippled the family although they occupied Lanherne on and off for another century. The most notable of these occupants was Mary, one of the most learned ladies of the seventeenth century, chiefly remembered for her translations from the latin.

The Arundells of Wardour

It was a second son of the family who moved out of Cornwall and continued the line. Thomas became a gentleman of Wolsey's household. He was knighted at the coronation of Anne Boleyn in 1533 and married a sister of Queen Catherine Howard. In 1535 Thomas was made a commissioner for the suppression of religious houses. He came under suspicion when his cousin led the 1549 Cornish rebellion, was in and out of the Tower for several years, and was eventually executed in the rivalries between Northumberland and Protector Somerset in the reign of Edward VI.

But he died a rich man, his fortune outstripping the senior branch of the family, and left Wardour Castle, just north-east of Shaftesbury, to his son Thomas. This young man was a great favourite of Queen Elizabeth and a gallant soldier; he was made a Count of the Holy Roman Empire for his courage fighting the Turks in Hungary. In 1605 Thomas was made first Baron Arundell of Wardour by James I. His son, the second baron, was another soldier who died of wounds received fighting for the King in the Civil War. In the same year, 1643, his wife Blanche won

A 1584 miniature of Thomas, first Lord Arundell of Wardour.

much fame for her defence of Wardour against the Parliamentary forces.

Next year her son, the third baron, recaptured Wardour. On the restoration of Charles II all the family estates were restored to him. He was one of the Catholic peers who negotiated the secret Treaty of Dover with France which was to reconcile the King with Rome. Later he was accused by Titus Oates of being one of the five 'popish lords' plotting against the King; was impeached and spent five years in the Tower. After 1688 and the accession of William and Mary he retired to private life

It was the seventh Lord Arundell who reunited the two lines by marrying Mary of Lanherne in 1739. Eventually the old house was given to a party of Carmelite nuns who in 1794 had fled from the perils of the French Revolution. So the house remains, still a nunnery, hidden behind its wall. In the village church across the way there are still the monuments and brasses to the great Arundells.

The title of Arundell of Wardour finally died out in 1944. The sixteenth Lord Arundell, a Catholic to the last, was a member of the Stock Exchange and in the 1939-45 war was a captain in the 2nd Wiltshire Regiment. He was taken

*Brasses in St Mawgan Church of Elizabethan
Arundells: left to right Cyssell and Jane (c.1580).*
From Dunkin. E.H.W. *Monumental Brasses of Cornwall.*

prisoner but repatriated, only to die in September 1944 at the age of 37. He had never married. Cornish travellers to London see the signpost to Tisbury on the A303, where there are more Arundell memorials. But Lanherne knows them no more.

Arundells of Trerice

The relationship between the Arundells of Trerice and Lanherne has never been clear, and indeed at one time the Trerice family claimed to be the senior line. The story emerges with some clarity in the reign of King Edward III

when Ralph Arundell married the heiress of Trerice. For three generations the family grew in prosperity if not in distinction until the reign of Edward IV.

In 1470 that Yorkist king had been briefly removed from his throne by Warwick the Kingmaker but he was back in England in 1471 and won back his throne at the Battle of Barnet. The Lancastrian Earl of Oxford fled to France and later landed in Cornwall and seized St Michael's Mount. John Arundell of Trerice, who had been knighted and made vice-admiral of Cornwall, was ordered by the king to recapture it. He was killed in a skirmish on the sands of Marazion, in front of the Mount. Sir John's original home had been at Efford, by the shore near Bude, but when it was prophesied that 'he should be slain in the sands' he had moved to Trerice!

His grandson, another Sir John, was more fortunate. Knighted at the Battle of the Spurs against the French in 1513, he became a favourite of the young Henry VIII and an Esquire of the Body. 'Jack of Tilbury', as he was known, advanced his favour with the king ten years later in a desperate sea battle which ended in his capturing a renowned Scottish pirate. Edward VI made him vice-admiral of the west and Queen Mary showed him further favours. Married twice and the father of twelve children, he died at the age of 67 a rich man.

His son, another John, was enabled by this wealth to build the delicious Elizabethan house at Trerice which is now a jewel in the National Trust's Cornish crown. It stands in a quiet valley in the parish of Newlyn East, not far from Newquay and only half a dozen miles south of that other Arundell house at Lanherne. His son-in-law was Richard Carew, Cornwall's first local historian, who paid the richest tribute to his father-in-law's virtues.

The son of his old age, yet another John, led an equally quiet life. He was a Member of Parliament a couple times, until the Civil War broke out when he was 65. Sir John at once offered his services to the King and was made governor of Pendennis, the castle which stands guard over

Trerice, the home of another Arundell branch; now a National Trust showpiece.

the entrance to Falmouth harbour. When the royal fortunes began to fade, first the Queen and then the Prince of Wales were sent west for safety. Sir John sheltered the Queen at Pendennis in 1644 and twenty months later was

The hall at Trerice.

until the royal cause was hopeless and only one day's food was left. Then terms were agreed and Sir John rode out at the head of his men, with flying colours, trumpets sounding, drums beating.

His eldest son had been killed leading a Royalist charge in the siege of Plymouth. Old Sir John was a ruined man, living in such poverty that he had to petition Cromwell for help. He died aged 79 without seeing his former guest at Pendennis, Charles II, restored to the throne. But the king remembered, and in 1644 raised his second son Richard, who had fought for the king at both Edgehill and Lansdown, to the peerage as Baron Arundell of Trerice. Four barons were to live quietly at Trerice, marrying well. The last, John, married a sister of the Earl of Strafford but died in 1773 without leaving an heir, and the title died out.

There were other junior branches of the family, like the Arundells of Tolverne on the left bank of the Fal. Apart from marrying regularly into the western gentry, they only distinguished themselves with a Thomas who, knighted by James I, ruined himself by trying to discover an imaginary island called Old Brazil off the American coast. A bastard son of Jack of Tilbury settled in Illogan. His great-grandson, Francis of Trengwainton, was a captain in the Parliamentary Army in the Civil War. An even more remote William Arundell who settled in East Cornwall married a daughter of Theodore Palaeologus, a descendant of the last emperors of Byzantium.

There are Arundells still in Cornwall, but none in their once great houses. Even the English branch has gone from Wardour.

host to the future King Charles II before he too took ship to safety.

In mid-March Fairfax, the Parliamentary general, was at the gates of Pendennis, demanding its surrender. Seventy-year old Sir John, for ever after known as 'Jack for the King', defied him, saying he would bury himself in the castle before delivering it up. For five months he held out

The Bassets of Tehidy

No traveller in West Cornwall has failed to see the great granite obelisk on the summit of Carn Brea. It commemorates Lord de Dunstanville, the most famous member of the Basset family. The first came to Cornwall in the Conqueror's time, and the last sold up the family house, Tehidy, in 1916.

Thurstan Basset fought with William at Hastings in 1066 and was sent to Cornwall as a soldier with Robert of Mortain. But they settled in Oxfordshire and not until Thomas Basset married the daughter and heiress of the Dunstanvilles of Tehidy did the family move to the West. With Tehidy they acquired the manors of Illogan, Redruth and Camborne, and so the richest mining land in the county. Their wealth came from owning the mineral-bearing land, rather than in any investment in mining.

Sir Ralph attended Edward I at Worcester in 1227, in the Welsh wars. In 1330 a Basset was given the market grant for Redruth, and licence to embattle Tehidy. Mining was already extensive, and enriching, in the area. The family held the castle on Carn Brea in the reign of Edward IV (1461-83), and regularly served as sheriffs of the county in early Tudor days.

A widowed Lady Basset married Lord Lisle, an important figure in Henry VIII's time. Her daughter Anne became a maid to his queen, Jane Seymour, who died giving birth to the future King Edward VI. During the next queen's reign, Anne of Cleves, it was rumoured that Anne Basset was among the favourites for the king's next choice of wife. But fortunately for her, perhaps, he married Catherine Howard.

In 1640 Sir Francis Basset, a jovial character much given to sport and hawking, bought St Michael's Mount. This meant that on the outbreak of the Civil War he was Lord and Captain of the Mount as well as Sheriff of Cornwall and vice-admiral of the Northern Shore. Intensely loyal to the king, he strengthened the fortifications of the Mount at his own expense and as the sheriff was busy throughout the war organising the finances for the royal forces, selling tin to raise money.

His brothers were more concerned with the actual fighting. Both held high rank in the Royalist army. Sir Thomas was at the skirmish at Chagford in 1643 when Sidney Godolphin was killed, and was a major-general in the Royalist forces which won the Battle of Stamford Bridge. His brother James was killed in a fight at Polsloe Bridge the same year. Thomas commanded a third of the army in the assault on Bristol. Francis was with the king at Boconnoc in 1644 after the successful campaign which defeated Essex. His Majesty knighted Francis, along with other Cornish gentlemen, and left him with the words, 'Now, Mr Sheriff, I leave Cornwall to you safe and sound'.

But it was not to be. Sir Francis died in September 1645.

Carn Brea; the castle (left) was held by the Basset family in the fifteenth century and the monument (right) commemorates the nineteenth century Basset who became Lord de Dunstanville. An 1859 drawing.

His brother Arthur took over command of the Mount and by December was pleading for help. Fairfax and Cromwell were advancing westwards. In February 1646 the Prince of Wales sailed from Pendennis to Scilly for safety, Sir Arthur escorting him. In April Sir Arthur, who had held both the Duke of Hamilton and Sir Richard Grenville as prisoners in the Mount, was forced to surrender it, leaving only Pendennis holding out.

The family fortunes, already hit by their wartime expenditure, suffered even more in the Commonwealth. Sir Francis's young heir had a spell in prison under Cromwell, though he had never borne arms for the king. By 1647 his fortunes were so reduced that he had to sell St Michael's Mount to John St Aubyn, one of the Parliamentary leaders. Recovery for the Bassets was to be a long, slow business.

Dolcoath, a nineteenth century drawing of one of the many mines found on Basset land which made the family fortune.

They laid low in the Whig supremacy of the early eighteenth century, but mining restored their fortunes once again. They owned Dolcoath and Cook's Kitchen, two of the richest mines in the county, and in one month alone the family income was £7040. By mid-century Pool mines were making £10 000 a year out of copper.

In 1734 John Pendarves Basset set about rebuilding Tehidy into an elegant Georgian mansion. No expense was

Tehidy, the family house as rebuilt in the eighteenth century.
Drawing from Borlase's *Natural History of Cornwall.*

spared either on house or the landscaping of the park. But he died of smallpox in 1739 aged only 25, leaving his widow with £100 000.

Tehidy passed to John's brother Francis, who was MP for Penryn 1766-9. To ship out the ores from his mines he began to create the little port of Portreath, on the north coast: it is still known as Basset's Cove.

His son, another Francis, made the Grand Tour as befits the heir of an affluent family. He continued his father's work at Portreath, and wrote a whole parcel of political treatises, ranging from relations with France to the state of Cornish agriculture. Francis, like most other landed gentlemen of the day, was also an enthusiastic borough-monger. For some years he battled with Lord Falmouth over the rights to Tregony and Truro, eventually agreeing that Falmouth should have Truro, and Basset Tregony. He reached a similar agreement with the Duke of Leeds, heir to the Godolphin lands, that they would not interfere with each other's boroughs of Penryn and Helston. Basset even fought a duel with Sir Christopher Hawkins, another borough-monger, over Parliamentary controls. They fired two shots each, both missed, and retired satisfied. Bassets also controlled the 36 voters of Bodmin.

In 1779, when Plymouth was threatened by the combined fleets of France and Spain in the Channel, young Francis led a party of his miners to the town and threw up earthworks and batteries for its protection. In reward he was made a baronet.

Next year he entered Parliament for his father's old seat, and promptly joined the party of Lord North. In 1782 he built defensive batteries on either side of Portreath. In 1782 he was the chief spirit in forming the Cornish Metal Company, trying to create a cartel with the Williams family of Angelsey to buy all the Cornish copper, a cartel which lasted until 1792. In 1785 he put down food riots in Redruth, swearing in fifty special constables and then arresting the ringleaders at crack of dawn in their beds. In 1796 Pitt made him Lord de Dunstanville (remembering

Lord de Dunstanville, an engraving by
G.H. Every from the Gainsborough portrait.

the heiress who had brought Tehidy to the Bassets so many centuries before).

The new lord, enjoying a 'princely income' (as the *Dictionary of National Biography* has it) from his mines, advanced mining interests in Cornwall and did much work for the welfare of miners. He was a liberal patron of literature and painting, an early patron of John Opie, the great Cornish painter, and a pall-bearer at his funeral in 1807. In 1809 he laid the first rail of one of the world's earliest iron railways, from Portreath to Dolcoath. His portrait still hangs in the museum of the Royal Institute of Cornwall in Truro.

Lord de Dunstanville died in 1835, at the age of 77, on his way to a session of Parliament, and was brought home to burial in Illogan church. A monument was raised to him on Carn Brea and the ninety-foot granite column still looks down across the mining country.

He was succeeded by his daughter Frances who became Baroness Basset of Stratton, one of his titles. She died in

1865, the last in the direct line. Tehidy and the estates passed to a nephew, Francis Henry Basset. With an income of £20 000 a year from his mines he set about enlarging the house in 1863, sparing no expense.

On his death in 1869 the estate again passed to a nephew, Arthur. Mining in west Cornwall was long past its peak, and incomes were dwindling, but this young man showed no regard. His twenty-first birthday in 1894 was celebrated with a lavish ball. He ignored falling income and increasing taxation to indulge his extravagant betting on horses. Tehidy grew shabby; his gardens increasingly neglected with the shortage of staff after 1914, and in 1916 the estate was split up and sold.

In 1919 Tehidy was bought as a county war memorial for use as a sanatorium. but within a few months was destroyed by fire. A new building was erected, lacking all the grace of the eighteenth-century house or its nineteenth-century enlargement. Only in 1989 did it cease to be a hospital.

After nine hundred years the Bassets have gone from Cornwall.

Tehidy in its last days as a sanatorium.

Merchant Princes: the Bolithos

Merchant princes of Cornwall, the Bolithos were called in 1885. They are remembered today mainly as bankers, but in the nineteenth century they were major smelters of tin, patriarchs of the industry. The Bolithos were also ship-owners, importers and dealers in hemp, cordage and tallow. They had a finger in every money-making pie in Cornwall.

The earliest records of the family go back to 1602 at Helston. They later became tanners and merchants at Penryn. By 1740 Thomas Bolitho was living at the Coombe, Madron, where his son, another Thomas (1765-1858), was born. This child was to be the founder of the family fortunes.

In 1781 Thomas leased, in partnership, lime pits at Chyandour, on the eastern edge of Penzance. This flourished until 1805 when the partners also took on the tin-smelting works close by. In 1807 Thomas and his brother William set up the Mount's Bay Commercial Bank, with its first offices in the smelting works. For the next century the names of Bolitho and Chyandour became inseparable, and the imposing house of Ponsandine on the road to Gulval became the Bolitho home.

Progress was steady. By 1815 they held three-sixteenths of Ding-dong, reputedly the oldest tin mine in Cornwall. By 1818 they were half-owners of Chyandour smelting works and built a blowing house there to produce the 'grain' tin required by the new tin plate industry. In the next ten years they built up a leading position in smelting. In 1828, when they were shareholders in three smelting houses, they bought two more, two-thirds of Calenick near Truro and the New Blowing House at St Austell.

The bank prospered. By 1834 it had premises in Market Jew Street, the principal thoroughfare of Penzance, and next year opened branches in St Just, St Ives, Hayle and Helston. In 1847 the bank took over the Penzance office of what had been the Western District Banking Co, and in 1879 took over the Helston Union Bank. Both had failed.

Thomas had three sons, Edward, born in 1804, Thomas Simon (1808-87) and William (1815-1895). All established separate homes in due course, Edward at Trewidden on the Land's End road, and William at Polwithen. Now Polwithen houses the St Clare School for Girls, and the estate is covered with houses.

Thomas Simon, who emerges as the most successful, moved about: he bought Penalverne and then Kenegie, all near Penzance, and then in 1866 he bought Trengwainton, a few miles north-west of Penzance. Originally owned by the Arundells of Trerice, the house had been built in 1814 by Sir Rose Price, son of a Jamaican sugar planter. Price began planting the trees which still grace the estate, but he was ruined by the Slave Emancipation Act of 1834.

In 1834 Edward, Thomas's son, was one of only five

Trengwainton, a drawing from the particulars of the sale in 1866 when T.S. Bolitho bought the property.
Today the house is embowered in trees and shrubs, but the Mount can still be seen from the terrace.

members of the pre-reform Penzance Town council to be elected to the new council. In 1837-8, the last year in which tin had to be presented on certain days in certain towns to Duchy officers to be coined, or taxed, the Bolithos were the biggest coiners in the county.

Edward was Mayor of Penzance in 1845, and his younger brother Thomas Simon, was mayor the following year, 1846. In that year the Prince Consort visited the works at Chyandour and ate beef steaks grilled on ingots of tin freshly drawn from the moulds. By now the smelters dominated the whole tin industry, as well as being investors in certain mines. It is noticeable that Bolitho names were absent from the lists of shareholders of unsuccessful mines; they were said to have 'a nose for tin'. By 1861 the Bolithos and the Williams families dominated the tin industry, with the Bolithos regarded as the patriarchs of the trade, the leaders of the 'ring' of smelters.

Patriarch was a good term, for old Thomas lived until he was 92, dying in 1858. His second son, Thomas Simon, was the new head of the family. In due course he became a

Justice of the Peace, Deputy Lieutenant of the county, High Sheriff and Deputy Warden of the Stannaries.

Edward's elder son, Edward Thomas (1831-45) died in his teens but the second son, Thomas Bedford (1835-1914) joined the business in due course as did Thomas Simon's son Thomas Robins (1840-1925). The progeny of the youngest brother, William, went on to carve careers for themselves in the army.

In 1871 the tin trade was on a wave of success. The Bolithos took a prominent share in Levant, the hugely successful mine at St Just. But in 1872 tin was found in Australia and, soon after, unsmelted tin was coming in along with ores from Bolivia. Bolitho began smelting this imported tin at Chyandour. By 1874 the less profitable Cornish mines were beginning to close and the family, never at a loss, began buying them up cheaply and selling off what was left.

In 1884, the year after the Chyandour tannery closed down, the Charleston smelting works were closed. But the family was still riding high. Thomas Bedford was High Sheriff and in 1885 the *Cornish Magazine and Devon Miscellany* described the family as the 'merchant princes' of Cornwall. They had the biggest fishing interest in most ports in the county (fortunes were being made in pilchards), extensive interests in farming (the coming of the railways had opened the rich broccoli trade) and few mines were without Bolitho money.

Thomas Simon died in 1887 and his son Thomas Robins followed him at Trengwainton and in the business. His cousin Thomas Bedford was elected MP for St Ives in that year, and held the seat until 1900. In 1890 he too was High Sheriff.

Tin was struggling. Wheal Sisters mine at Lelant was closed, although the family had lost £2700 in the previous fourteen years trying to keep it alive. In 1891 the principal Cornish smelters amalgamated and closed all but three works. Chyandour was one of the survivors. Malayan tin was beginning to flood the market, depressing Cornish tin.

Thomas Robins Bolitho stands beside his wife in her donkey cart.

Banking was also suffering. In 1889 Bolithos amalgamated their Mount's Bay Bank with the East Cornwall Bank, in which they had already acquired shares. In 1890 further amalgamations swallowed up banks right across the county (even Hodge & Co of Devonport, Devon) to become the Consolidated Bank of Cornwall. Thomas

The funeral cortège of T.R. Bolitho passing the lodge in 1925.

Bedford Bolitho MP played a leading part in all these moves, and when in 1905 Consolidated was taken over by Barclays, Thomas and three other Bolithos were among the local directors. The family's wealth grew. In 1897 Thomas Robins enlarged Trengwainton to its present size, and built the wide carriage drive. For a record fifty-five years he was Master of the Western Foxhounds. The family's charitable gifts to Penzance were generous; almshouses, a sailors' institute, a new convalescent home, much of the cost of a new park. In spite of all these gifts, they acquired a local reputation as hard-headed businessmen with little sympathy for the hard-pressed. The smelting works at Chyandour finally closed in 1912. With the outbreak of war two years later, and the closure of the London Metal Market, tin prices really collapsed. The Bolitho Bank spent almost £3000 buying black tin in their efforts to reduce unemployment. The industry struggled on for a few years after the war, but survived only in one or two mines.

Col. Sir Edward Bolitho as Lord Lieutenant, escorting King George VI on a visit to Cornwall.

Thomas Bedford died in 1915, leaving only daughters. Thomas Robins died in 1925, and Trengwainton passed to his nephew, Lieut. Col. E.H.W. Bolitho, Royal Field Artillery (1882-1969). The colonel's father, second son of Thomas Simon, had made his career in the Royal Navy, retiring as a captain. Sir Edward, as he became in 1953, gave his life on his retirement from the army to public affairs: High Sheriff 1931, a hard-working Lord Lieutenant 1936-62 and even more hard-working as Chairman of the County Council, 1941-52.

Major Simon Bolitho.

At Trengwainton he set about the park, creating the magnificent garden we know today. He sought the advice of other great Cornish gardeners, J.C. Williams of Caerhays and George Johnstone of Trewithen. He took a share in Kingdon Ward's plant-collecting expeditions to Assam and Burma. Some of the rhododendrons and magnolias in the garden resulted from this venture. These species are still the backbone of the garden but there are shrubs from every corner of the globe. In one area a variety of specimen trees have been planted in honour of royal events, two of them by members of the royal family.

Sir Edward was succeeded by his son, Major Simon Bolitho, Grenadier Guards (1916-1991). Like his father he was a regular soldier, and even as his father was twice wounded in World War One, so Simon was twice wounded in World War Two. After that he saw service in Palestine. He was Lieut. Col. of the Duke of Cornwall's Light Infantry (1957-60), and High Sheriff of Cornwall in 1956. He became a Deputy Lieutenant in 1964 and was a county councillor from 1953 to 1967. When Simon died he was followed by his eldest son, Edward, born in 1955. Another regular soldier Edward was by 1994 Lieut. Col. commanding the 1st Grenadier Guards.

Pilchards and tin, the old backbone of the Cornish economy, and the foundations of the family fortune, are both shadows of their former greatness. In 1961, Sir Edward made the garden over to the National Trust, while the family maintain the house.

15

Boscawens,
The Lords Falmouth

The Boscawens owe their eminence to fortunate marriages which brought them lands rich in tin and copper, and their Puritan faith which in the Civil War led them to support Parliament and, in the next century, a natural progression to the Whigs. Indeed the eighteenth century, the years of the Whig supremacy, was the period of their greatness. In the early years the head of the family was a great political manager in Cornwall and became Viscount Falmouth, while three of his sons were generals and the fourth an admiral in the Navy.

The family originated at Boscawen Ros, in St Buryan parish near the Land's End, and they still have a rose in their coat of arms, even though 'ros' in Cornish is moorland, and Boscawen means the humble dwelling by the elder tree. In 1335 John de Boscawen married Joan of Tregothnan, at the confluence of the Fal and Truro rivers, and the family has been settled there ever since.

Other fortunate marriages brought in more land west of the rivers around Chacewater and Gwennap which in time turned out to be rich in copper, but the family lived quietly. At the coronation of Henry VII a Boscawen paid a fine of 5d to avoid going to court to receive a knighthood, and his grandson did the same thing at the coronation of Mary Tudor. The family, it has been said, was wealthy but unambitious and undistinguished.

Hugh Boscawen (1578-1641) began the family's climb in Stuart times. He married a Rolle, of the Devon family whose wealth was matched only by the Russells. He became Recorder of Truro and began forging the family's links with the borough. Hugh was a member for the county in 1626 when Parliament impeached Buckingham and opposed the new king. Boscawen was aware that revenues from mining were falling under the Stuarts, and that the county's trade was suffering. He too was a Puritan, though like all his family he had no desire to leave the Church of England. But he died in 1641, just before the start of the Civil War, leaving four sons of whom the eldest, Nicholas, was only nineteen.

Nicholas at once joined the Parliamentary Army with a regiment of horse, a demonstration of the family's devotion to the cause, only to be killed when he was twenty-two. He was buried in Westminster Abbey (after the Restoration his remains were dug up and flung in a common pit). His younger brothers were barely of age when the war ended, but both Hugh (1625-1701) and Charles were members of Commonwealth parliaments. Like most of the Parliamentary gentlemen of Devon and Cornwall, they became tired of the Commonwealth rule and played their part in supporting General Monck at the Restoration.

Hugh inherited Tregothnan, which he rebuilt in the 1650s. Maybe the old house had suffered during the Royalist sequestration in the war years There he was able to entertain his cousin, Celia Fiennes, on her celebrated ride around England in 1698 and she found the house very pleasant and civilised, complete even with a little smoking

Tregothnan, the great house of the Boscawens, rebuilt in the 1650s and again in the 1820s, seen here in 1976.

room. He had lived to regret helping to bring back the Stuarts, and played his part in bringing over William III. When he died in 1701 he was succeeded by his brother Edward's son, another Hugh. Edward had been an MP for Truro in each of the Parliaments of Charles II, and became a rich merchant.

Hugh (c.1666-1734) became the leading Whig politician of his day in Cornwall. He controlled Tregony and Truro, had one seat at St Michael's Mount, and influence in Penryn. He was a Member of Parliament continuously from 1702, and spent a lot of money in the Whig cause. He could afford to, the mines were booming and in 1700 Boscawen was receiving £1000 a year from the copper mines. Like most Cornish landowners the Boscawens played no part in the mining operations; they simply leased rights on their land to the adventurers.

When George I came to the throne, Hugh became Controller of the Royal Household, and the great days of the Whig supremacy had begun. He became a Privy Councillor, Lord Warden of the Stannaries, had a fashionable house in Albemarle Street, and became peevish when he had to wait so long for the peerage he aimed at. But finally he was created Viscount Falmouth in 1720.

On the accession of George II, Hugh's wife did her utmost, even trying bribery, to become a lady of the bedchamber to the 'blatantly sexual and earthy' Queen

Caroline. The Falmouths had a large family, with three of their sons becoming generals in the army. These were the days when promotion was by purchase. One son, George, saw service at Dettingen in 1643 in which the Army was commanded by George II, the last time an English monarch led a battle. He was at Fontenoy two years later under the command of the king's son, the young Duke of Cumberland.

But it was the Admiral, Edward (1711-61), who became the most distinguished of all the Boscawens. He was described as 'Pitt's great admiral', who said to him 'other officers... make difficulties, you find expedients'. He had the reputation of always going baldheaded for the enemy. Horace Walpole, son of the great Whig Prime Minister who of course knew the Boscawens well and moved in the same fashionable London circles, called him 'this most obstinate member of an obstinate family'.

He joined the *Superbe* at the age of fourteen and was to serve mainly in the West Indies and the Mediterranean before becoming a lieutenant six years later. By 1739 he was in command of the 20-gun *Shoreham*, refitting at Jamaica, when Admiral Vernon sailed against Portobello. He obtained leave to serve on the flagship as a volunteer. He acquitted himself well on a shore expedition, and two years later when Vernon repeated this foray, against Cartagena, Boscawen was there in the *Shoreham*. Again he led a shore expedition with remarkable success, one of the few achievements in a bungled affair.

On return to England he was in 1743 given command of the 60-gun *Dreadnought*. One night, he was wakened with the news that two French ships were bearing down on them. 'What shall we do?'. 'Do', roared Boscawen, 'fight'em of course'. A few weeks later he made the first capture of the war, a French frigate, and his nickname 'Old Dreadnought' was born.

In 1747 Anson took command of a fleet in which Boscawen was senior captain in the *Namur*. Anson captured a complete French fleet, and £300 000 worth of treasure in the First Battle of Finisterre; Boscawen fought like a lion, and in reward became rear-admiral of the red. He was thirty-six, the youngest admiral in the Royal Navy, and given a remarkable post as commander-in-chief of H.M. Forces by sea and land in the East Indies. He failed in the objectives given him, but came home with an enhanced reputation.

'Old Dreadnought' or 'Captain Ned'; Edward Boscawen the great admiral. A painting by Reynolds.

Boscawen held various shore appointments, chief among them being a lord commissioner of the Admiralty under Anson. He had been MP for Truro since 1742, and was able to take his seat rather more, and be with his wife in their house at 2 St James's Square. From his exploits afloat he had taken three enemy guns, sunk them in the pavement outside the house and made them the base of lamp posts. To his wife, who was a fashionable lady renowned then and in her long widowhood for her salons which attracted poets, painters and writers, he was 'dashing Captain Ned'. She is credited with having originated, with her friend Mrs Montagu, the blue-stocking assemblies which would substitute the pleasures of conversation for the inescapable rubbers of whist.

Boscawen, promoted vice-admiral in 1755, was two years later at sea as second-in-command to Admiral Hawke of the main fleet. In 1758 he became admiral of the blue. The fleet was divided to watch the French, Hawke (that other great Cornish admiral) off Brest and Boscawen off Toulon. When Boscawen had to retire to Gibraltar in 1759 he set watch in the straits for the Toulon fleet trying to escape the Mediterranean to link up with the Brest fleet.

They did get through, with Boscawen in pursuit. He caught and smashed half the Toulon fleet, and the other half took refuge in Portuguese waters, in Lagos Bay. Ignoring the laws of neutrality Boscawen went straight in to the attack, and the French fleet to all practical purposes ceased to exist. Three months later Hawke smashed the Brest Fleet in Quiberon Bay. The new-born British Empire was saved, and the nation rejoiced. Boscawen was made a Privy Councillor and, more valuable, a General of Marines which brought in a handsome income. He did not live long to enjoy his new fame; typhoid claimed him in 1761.

The admiral's elder brother, Hugh (1706-1782), one of the family's generals, became the second Viscount Falmouth in 1734. He was Captain of the Yeoman of the Guard but the family had lost, not without rancour, the leadership of the Westcountry Whigs to the Edgcumbes. In 1774 he sold three Cornish seats to the Tory Lord North, who offered £7500. Falmouth demanded guineas, which North regarded as rather shabby. The second viscount died without children in 1782 and the title passed to the admiral's family.

The admiral's eldest son, sometime MP for Truro, died abroad in 1774, and his second son, a naval officer, was drowned in Port Royal, Jamaica in 1769. So his third son, George Evelyn (1758-1808) succeeded his uncle as the third viscount. As a soldier he was present at the skirmish at Lexington when the first blood was shed in what became the American War of Independence. Two years later he was on easier ground, pacifying a mob of angry miners in Truro.

On his death in 1808 he was followed by his son Edward (1787-1841). He left the army, and had to give up his year-old Parliamentary representation of Truro. But he continued to be assiduous in his Parliamentary duties, fighting the Whigs with venom. The Reform Bill, he said, would destroy the Church of England. Later on the liberal politics of George Canning infuriated him. He seems to have been a cantankerous character, and was second to Lord Winchelsea in his duel with the Duke of Wellington.

At the coronation of Prinny, George IV, he was created the first Earl of Falmouth, and celebrated by rebuilding Tregothnan, employing William Wilkins, architect of the National Gallery, to produce a 'Tudor' castle in the picturesque style. His son, George Henry (1811-52), who became the second earl in 1841, was also the last, for he died childless. He too enlarged the house, and was a considerable scholar.

Tregothnan passed to his cousin Evelyn (1819-89), whose major contribution was to start laying out the gardens, planting camellias and some of the huge rhododendrons brought back from the Himalayas in 1848. He was also a most successful racehorse owner, winning the Derby, the St Leger and the Two Thousand Guineas twice, and the Oaks and the Thousand Guineas four times. His magpie colours

The ninth Viscount Falmouth, in his uniform as Lord Lieutenant, with Lady Falmouth, unveiling a tablet commemorating his great naval forebear at Culdrose Naval Air Station in 1985.

Left: *Evelyn, Viscount Falmouth, an enthusiastic racehorse owner who never placed a bet.* From the *Cornish Magazine* of 1898-9.

Right: *Fred Archer, the great jockey who regularly rode for Lord Falmouth.* A Spy cartoon from *Vanity Fair.*

were legendary, as was his long partnership with the great Fred Archer, his jockey. But he never placed a single bet.

His son, Evelyn Edward Thomas (1847-1918), who succeeded his father as seventh viscount, was a regular soldier, retiring as a major-general and being colonel of the family regiment, the Coldstream Guards. He became Deputy Warden of the Stannaries in 1911.

The eighth viscount, E. H. J. Boscawen (1887-1962), broke away from family tradition by becoming a leading engineer. He was an honorary fellow and chairman of the Imperial College of Science and Technology, on the executive committee of the National Physics Laboratory 1935-40, and chairman of various government committees. From 1925 until 1937 he was a member, later alderman, of London County Council. During the Second World War he was head of division of the mysteriously-named R & E Division of the Ministry of Home Security, which sounds

remarkably like David Audley's outfit in the Anthony Price spy thrillers.

His eldest son, Evelyn, was commissioned in the Coldstream Guards on coming down from Cambridge, but was killed in action at Calais in 1940. So his younger brother, George Hugh, a captain in the Coldstream Guard from 1940 to 1945, became the ninth and present viscount. In Cornwall he was made Deputy Lieutenant in 1968 and became Lord Lieutenant in 1977, a title he relinquished on his 75th birthday in 1994.

Walter Tregellas in his 1884 *Worthies of Cornwall* rather unkindly says that distinguished Cornish families all yielded more than one man of note, but this can hardly be said of the Boscawens. Of course the admiral stands out, but they do present a picture of a rich and sometimes idiosyncratic family that has served the county well. St Michael Penkivell Church, rebuilt by Street in the 1860s and heavily decorated, is full of their memorials but Pevsner was not impressed by any of them; the family has, in his words 'not had a great confidence in monumental memorials'.

Carew Poles of Antony

Sir Richard Carew, author of the Survey of Cornwall, *a portrait hanging in Antony House.*

Carews and Poles, two of the oldest families in the West of England, came together at Antony as the result of an eighteenth-century alliance. The Carews arrived first, in the fifteenth century, but the family goes back to Norman times.

They are descended from the Carews of Carew Castle, in Pembrokeshire, and had a lively beginning. The daughter of a Welsh ruler, so beautiful that she was known as Helen of Wales, married a Norman baron in 1100 and bore him five children. But a Welshman, inflamed by her beauty, captured both the castle and her, and she bore him two children. Six years later the Norman recaptured her, and killed the Welshman in battle. The Norman died a year later; the lady married another Norman and bore him more children.

A son of the first marriage inherited Carew Castle and took the name Carew. From him are descended the whole scattered tribe, including the Cornish branch, but even their beginnings at Antony are complicated.

Sir Hugh Courtenay, son of the Earl of Devon, married the heiress of Antony. He lived at Boconnoc, owning a number of manors in both Cornwall and Devon, but he was executed after the Battle of Tewkesbury in 1471. All his possessions passed to his only daughter Joan. Her first husband was Sir Nicholas Carew of Haccombe in Devon.

When he died and his wife inherited she quarrelled with her eldest son, who struck her. For this insult she dispossessed him, and divided her land between her four younger sons. Alexander, the youngest, inherited Antony and the estate came down through a succession of sons to

Sir Wymond Carew who died in 1549, having sired nineteen children. The eldest, Thomas, married a daughter of the Sir Richard Edgcumbe who built Mount Edgcumbe House, and later bought the manor of Sheviock. Thomas died in 1564, and the estate passed to his eldest son, Richard (1555-1620).

At Oxford Richard was a friend of Philip Sidney and with him met the leading literary people of the day. This quiet scholarly man served his county in local affairs, as had his predeccessors, as sheriffs and Members of Parliament. In 1612 he built the little harbour and pilchard cellars at Portwrinkle, in Sheviock parish, to serve the fishing industry which had moved out of Plymouth to avoid Elizabeth's local taxation. But his great joy was in the fish pond he built in the valley in front of his old house, and in his books.

From Oxford he went into the Middle Temple where he was able to keep his literary friends, especially William Camden, the leading antiquary of the age and the writer of the magisterial survey of all England. Richard Carew was among the very first fellows of the London Society of Antiquaries, and he in turn wrote his celebrated *Survey of Cornwall*, published in 1602. It is one of the first surveys of English counties that were beginning to appear, reflecting the new pride of the English in their homeland. Carew's survey gives us our earliest view of Cornwall, its people, their houses and their occupations. It is quoted in virtually every book about the county. Richard also had a number of long poems published, typical of their times.

In 1578 he married Juliana, daughter of John Arundell of Trerice, one of the grandees of Cornwall. Their eldest son, Richard (1580-1643) travelled with his uncle George Carew on embassies to Germany and Sweden, and was also a writer. He succeeded his father in 1620. By his first marriage this Richard was related to Strode of Plympton, Sir John Eliot of St Germans, and John Pym, all leaders of Parliament in the struggle against the king. Richard was a Puritan like his father, and a Member of Parliament. But

his great interest was in natural curiosities, strange health cures, and his garden.

He was never sure of his opposition to the king, and even accepted, possibly bought, a baronetcy from Charles. When the war started he was placed on Cornish committees supporting Parliament, but the problem of loyalty was solved by his death in 1643.

His eldest son, Alexander (1609-44), was a much more convinced Parliament man and as a member had voted for the execution of Strafford. On the outbreak of war he was made governor of Drake's Island in Plymouth Sound, a key point in the town's defences during its long strugle against the king. But as the war seemed to be swinging in

The library at Antony House, showing the portrait of Sir Alexander Carew. This portrait was cut from the fame after his execution, and only later stitched back on.

the king's favour, Alexander wavered; he entered into negotiations with the Royalists to turn the island over to them, and was arrested on the island beach. He was shipped off to London for trial and execution in 1644.

His portrait at Antony House has at some time been cut from its frame, and later stitched back. The family legend is that it was cut out when he attempted to betray the Parliamentary cause, and only replaced after the Restoration.

Richard's half-brother, John (1622-60), never wavered in his Parliamentary zeal; he was one of those who signed the death warrant of King Charles and on the Restoration was summoned to London to stand trial. Though his friends urged him to flee the country he went, was inevitably

found guilty and was executed. It is typical of the division caused in Cornish loyalties by the Civil War; two brothers executed, one by each side.

Alexander's son, Sir John (1635-92), was a moderate Presbyterian but was one of the Cornish members of Parliament who worked for and welcomed the return of Charles II. When he died in 1692 his son, Sir William (1689-1743), was a convinced supporter of the Stuarts. He was so determined a Jacobite that he was imprisoned in the Citadel at Plymouth during 1715. There was good reason; a portrait of Sir Watkin Williams-Wynn at Antony bears the legend that the two men had exchanged portraits as a mutual pledge, Carew to raise Cornwall for the Pretender and Williams-Wynn to raise Wales.

Torpoint Ferry in 1890, when it was still owned by the Pole Carew family.

But generally Sir John laid low in those Whiggish times, concentrating on cultivating his garden and planning a new house. It stands about a mile south-west of the old Tudor house. He had been planning this since 1710, in anticipation of his marriage to the heiress of the fourth Earl of Coventry, who had married an Edgcumbe. They were married in 1714 after some bargaining about the settlement, but the house was begun in 1718 and completed in a couple of years. Pevsner calls it 'the best example of its date in Cornwall'.

John died in 1743 and his son Sir Coventry was only to enjoy the house for five years. On his death the estate and title passed to a son of the Sir Alexander executed by Parliament in 1644, but the baronetcy was extinct by 1799. Other cousins held the estate, which passed to a Devon cousin in 1771.

Reginald Pole (1753-1835) may or may not have been related to the great Poles and Dukes of Suffolk of early Tudor days, but he was still a member of a rich and powerful East Devon family.

His father is described as being of Stoke Damerell, the present Devonport just across the Tamar from Antony, and it is probable that he lived at Mount Wise. Reginald's brother Charles Morice joined the Navy, became an admiral and a knight, and for twelve years was an MP for Plymouth.

Reginald was eighteen when he came to Antony, and changed his name to Pole Carew. He travelled extensively in Europe between 1775 and 1781, came home and entered Parliament as MP for Penryn, and in 1784 married the heiress of the Hon. John Yorke, fourth son of the Earl of Hardwicke, a leading politician and a family much in the smart world. He often stayed with his wife's parents at the fashionable spa of Sunninghill and bought a London house just off Berkeley Square.

But he was still much at Antony and added West Antony and Tregantle to the family estates. He began cleaning out the formal garden of the last Sir John and brought in Repton to advise on laying out the new style 'natural and picturesque' park that we know today.

The town of Torpoint had started to grow on the edge of the Antony estate in Sir Coventry's time, profiting from the rapid growth of Plymouth Dock around the new Dockyard. Reginald began really to plan and develop it, laying the foundations of what is now the twelfth largest town in Cornwall, and still growing. He was a leading spirit in creating the turnpike from Tregantle to Torpoint which replaced the old southern main road into Cornwall from Mount Edgcumbe. With the Earl of Mount Edgcumbe he launched the Torpoint Ferry in 1790, which was carrying the Cornish mails by 1794 and became a steam chain ferry in 1834.

Reginald died in 1835 to be followed by his son Joseph, who died within three years. The estate passed to his half-brother William (1811-88), interested in farming and an MP for East Cornwall. William's son Reginald (1849-1924) went into the army and was already a distinguished soldier when he succeeded to Antony in 1888. He took part in the famous march from Kabul to Kandahar, was a staff officer in the occupation of Burma, took part in the Battle of Tel-el-Kebir and commanded a division in the Boer War. He came out of the army as Lieutenant-General Sir Reginald Pole Carew, and was MP for Bodmin from 1910 to 1916. In the First World War he was Inspector-General of the Territorial Army, finally retiring in 1916 after a severe riding accident.

When he died in 1924 the estate passed to his son John, born in 1922. In 1926, at the age of twenty-four and a serving officer in the Coldstream Guards, John inherited the Pole baronetcy and changed the order of his name, becoming Sir John Carew Pole. John was to remove the ostentatious Victorian wing his father had added to the house, and the parterre garden in front, restoring the Repton idea. With advice from famous Cornish gardeners, J. C. Williams of Caerhays, George Johnstone of Trewithen and Sir Edward Bolitho of Trengwainton, he began to establish the glorious woodland walks which stretch right and his son Richard took over the big house. Sir John died in 1993.

Richard, born in 1938, has served in the Coldstream Guards like his father and grandfather. He too has been High Sheriff and Chairman of the Finance Committee of the County Council, from which he retired on his father's death.

So for five hundred years the family has been at Antony, playing no great part in national affairs but serving the county and caring for their estate. With two sons, the present Sir Richard is continuing the family traditions.

Sir Reginald Pole Carew, the distinguished general. A Spy cartoon from *Vanity Fair.*

down to the banks of the Lynher. In the Second World War he commanded the 2nd Devonshire Regiment in the Normandy landings and retired as a colonel.

Sir John has played a considerable part in Cornish affairs, being High Sheriff, Chairman of the County Council from 1952 to 1961 and Lord Lieutenant from 1962 until 1977. Concerned about the future upkeep of the house he made it, and the immediate gardens, over to the National Trust in 1961 with a suitable endowment. In 1983 he moved from Antony to a smaller house on the estate,

Sir John Carew Pole and his heir Richard, in front of the north facade of Antony House, 1986.

Edgcumbes
of Mount Edgcumbe

Two marriages to heiresses, and loyalty to the right political party in different centuries, brought the Edgcumbes fame and fortune.

William Edgcumbe, a farmer from Edgcumbe, midway between Tavistock and Launceston on the Devon bank of the Tamar, married Hilaria the heiress of Cotehele in 1353. She brought with her a great house and estate, and their descendants ranked with the leading Cornish gentry.

Their great-grandson Richard rebuilt Cotehele into the house we know today. He was a Lancastrian in the Wars of the Roses. In 1483, when the Yorkist Richard III usurped the throne and murdered the true heir and his brother in the Tower, Richard Edgcumbe joined the other gentlemen of the West at Exeter in proclaiming Henry Tudor, the Earl of Richmond, as king. Richmond did appear briefly in Plymouth Sound and landed at Cawsand, but prudently re-embarked and went back to his exile in Brittany. The rising had already failed, the Western gentlemen scattered, and Henry Bodrugan, a leading Cornish Yorkist, pursued Richard Edgcumbe to Cotehele. Richard escaped by throwing his cap into the Tamar to make his pursuers think he had leapt into the river, and lived to get away himself to Brittany.

But he was back with Henry Tudor in 1485, fought valiantly at Bosworth and was knighted on the field by the victorious King Henry VII. Richard was very close to the new king, who made him comptroller of his household, heaped many favours and manors on him, and employed him in various embassies abroad. On one such errand to Brittany he died, in 1489, and was buried at Morlaix where a monument was raised to him.

His son Piers (1469-1539) followed the example of his great-great-grandfather and married an heiress, this time Joan Durnford of Stonehouse. She not only brought him the Stonehouse lands, covering both sides of the mouth of the Tamar, but also the old Valletort manor house in Plymouth, where her forbears had played quite a part. Sir Piers followed their example and seems to have lived at the Valletort house as well as at the Stonehouse manor. He spent a lot of money on his new estates, was sheriff of Devon three times and is frequently mentioned in the Plymouth town records.

Not that Piers neglected Cornwall; he added the great hall at Cotehele and invested heavily in some new-fangled ideas in tin-mining, joining with a friend in bringing in German engineers. He also commanded two hundred Cornishmen in the army sent against the Pilgrimage of Grace, that northern revolution, in 1539. But most significantly, he received a licence to enclose a deer park on his land across the Tamar, in Maker parish.

The son, Sir Richard (1499-1562), went further. He built a new house in the deer park between 1549 and 1553, and henceforward house and park were known as Mount Edgcumbe. It was a revolutionary design, foursquare with a tower at each corner. A year after the house was completed Sir Richard held a great party there at which,

*The garden front of Cotehele, the
early home of the Edgcumbes.*

The Great Hall at Cotehele.

according to Jewitt's *History of Plymouth*, he entertained some Spanish grandees. At this party was the Duke of Medina Sidonia who, when he later commanded the Spanish Armada against England, declared that he wanted Mount Edgcumbe as his reward!

Richard's son Piers (1536-1607) was a Member of Parliament for most of Elizabeth's Parliaments and his Aunt Margaret a maid of honour to Queen Elizabeth. He was a sheriff of Devon (Mount Edgcumbe was part of Devon until 1844) and a partner in privateering ventures against Spain in the 1580s. His son Richard (1565-1639) was knighted at the coronation of James 1 in 1603.

Throughout the Civil Wars Mount Edgcumbe was held for the king by Colonel Piers Edgcumbe (1609-1666) just as neighbouring Plymouth held out for Parliament. The town's garrison raided the estate and house several times without capturing it. When Fairfax and Cromwell advanced into the West in 1646, Richard arranged the surrender of Mount Edgcumbe and the East Cornwall

27

The bedroom in which Charles I is said to have slept at Cotehele. As the house has been largely unoccupied since Queen Anne's time, its furnishings are still of that period.

Royalists through the cloak and dagger activities of Phillipa Coryton. As a result the estate escaped lightly in the fines imposed on the Royalist landowners at the end of the war.

On the Restoration Colonel Edgcumbe's son Richard (1639-1688) was knighted, and entertained Charles II twice when the King visited Plymouth. But his son Richard (1680-1758) was no Jacobite. As a boy he wrote elegant latin verse to welcome William III when the Dutchman turned out King James. A Member of Parliament like so many of his predecessors, he became a great friend of the Whig Robert Walpole and one of his strongest supporters.

Edgcumbe was rewarded when Walpole finally achieved power in 1720 by being made a Lord of the Treasury and in 1727 Vice-Treasurer of Ireland. He was important to Walpole because he had taken over from Lord Falmouth as manager of the Whig influence in Devon and Cornwall, able to control or buy a number of seats. In 1730 as chairman of committee of the whole House of Commons, Edgcumbe manipulated a crucial debate in Walpole's favour. When Walpole's rule collapsed in 1742 Edgcumbe was made a peer to render him immune to questioning by the House of Commons on his management of the Cornish seats.

So Lord Edgcumbe retired to his estates and began converting Mount Edgcumbe park into a landscape reflecting the 'natural' taste of the day, complete with follies and elegant drives. He became Lord Lieutenant of Cornwall in 1744, and in spite of being so deeply involved in the political corruption of his age, was held to be an honest and worthy man in all other respects. He was said to be a favourite of George II because he was the only man at court shorter than the monarch.

Richard was the first patron of Joshua Reynolds, whose father was the schoolmaster at Plympton, one of the Edgcumbe boroughs, and it was at dinner at Mount Edgcumbe, when the younger son, Commodore Edgcumbe, had brought his friend Captain (later the famous admiral) Keppel, that Reynolds's passage to Italy, so vital in his development, was arranged as Keppel's guest.

Lord Edgcumbe's eldest son Richard (1716-1761) was a boyhood friend of Reynolds and later a great friend of Walpole's son, the celebrated Horace of Strawberry Hill. Dick Edgcumbe, as he is remembered, had a house near Strawberry Hill and Horace found him charming, witty and elegant. Dick was a thorough man of his times, a poet and amateur artist, a gambler who 'threw away his twenty guineas a day at White's', was acquainted with all the best people, and kept the actress Anne Franks as his mistress. He had four children by her, and never married.

From his Grand Tour Dick brought back the orange trees for which the first Lord Camelford, an amateur architect and member of the Twickenham circle, designed the

Orangery at Mount Edgcumbe. Dick held various seats in Parliament 'to keep the family interest warm', became a Lord of the Admiralty and later Comptroller of the Royal Household. When Dick's father died he became the second baron and Lord Lieutenant of Cornwall, but he died three years later, at the age of 45.

The title passed to his brother George (1721-95). A naval officer, he was made post captain at the age of 23 (the Navy was always a Whig service, and George's father an influential Whig). He was MP for Fowey (1747-61) as well as a serving officer, but saw plenty of action. In 1756 he was a commodore when he joined Byng for the abortive action off Minorca which led to Byng's execution, but Edgcumbe was not among the captains recalled. He captured a number of quite rich prizes in his time, was with Boscawen in American waters in 1758 and later that year commanded the *Hero* in Admiral Hawke's victory in Quiberon Bay.

George continued at sea after inheriting the peerage, and was made admiral in 1762. He was Port Admiral Plymouth (1766-70) and no doubt lived at home. He continued the work on the gardens started by his father, but patriotically, in 1779 when a combined French and Spanish fleet threatened a landing in Plymouth Sound, he felled all the trees bordering the sea to make way for gun emplacements. As it happened, the clearance made way for the formal gardens we enjoy today, and two years later, on a visit by George III, Baron Edgcumbe was created Viscount Mount Edgcumbe in recognition of his service and in reward for the sacrifice of his trees.

During the century Plymouth had been developing fast as a naval base, with the Dockyard growing apace at Plymouth Dock – later Devonport. Stonehouse, between Plymouth and Dock, became valuable property. The first Lord Edgcumbe sold to the government, in 1758, land on the shores of Stonehouse Creek for a naval hospital, and in 1780 the admiral sold them land on the shores of Mill Bay for a Royal Marine barracks. He had in 1773 built

The view towards Devonport from the garden at Mount Edgcumbe.

Mount Edgcumbe c.1830.

Stonehouse Bridge with St Aubyn, who owned Devonport, and then began to build elegant houses in Durnford Street for the growing numbers of naval officers and professional men concerned with the new Dockyard. From this grew a whole new residential area, all leased, which made a great deal of money for the family.

The family interest in politics was fading; indeed was changing sides, for Lord Edgcumbe sold three parliamentary seats to the Tory Lord North. North complained that Edgcumbe was going to sell the seats for £12 500 but finally demanded, and got, £15 000! On a second visit of King George, Edgcumbe became the first Earl of Mount Edgcumbe.

His son Richard (1764-1839), the second earl, was a gifted amateur of the arts, writing an opera, the prologue to a play, composing verse and taking part in the amateur theatricals so popular at the great houses such as Saltram. With his wife Lady Sophia, daughter of the Earl of Buckingham, he continued to develop the gardens. He also sold to the Admiralty more land at Stonehouse, as the site of the Royal William Victualling Yard.

The third earl, Ernest Augustus (1797-1861), built Winter Villa at Stonehouse in 1856, partly to improve his ill-health and partly for his wife, who disliked the winters at Mount Edgcumbe and sought the social life of Plymouth. Among his visitors at Mount Edgcumbe were the Grand Duke Michael of Russia, the Duke of Clarence (later William IV), and Queen Victoria (twice). His son William Henry (1833-1917) was even more favoured, entertaining the Emperor Frederick of Germany, the Emperor Napoleon III of France, Empress Elizabeth of Austria and the King of Sweden.

William in fact was much in favour at the English court, aide-de-camp to Victoria, travelling companion to the Prince of Wales and a close friend; the Prince regularly visited Mount Edgcumbe. Locally William, when Viscount Valletort, had won the Plymouth Parliamentary seat as a Conservative in 1859 and made the only break in the Liberal stranglehold in 35 years. He had to give up his seat when his father died in 1861. As fourth earl he was Lord Chamberlain of the Royal Household for a couple of years, Lord Lieutenant and Vice-Admiral of Cornwall, chairman of the committee for the building of Truro Cathedral and the first Chairman of the County Council on its establishment in 1889.

Amateur theatricals in 1788, a painting by James Roberts showing the 'neat little beau' Richard Edgcumbe (left) with Sir William Russell and Lady Caroline Spencer

His only son Piers (1865-1944) had the melancholy fate of seeing Mount Edgcumbe House reduced to ruined walls in the German blitz on Plymouth in 1941. Fire destroyed nearly all the pictures, including many by Reynolds, and the family moved to Cotehele, its early home. Piers had no children, so on his death the title passed to Kenelm, descended from a son of the second earl.

Kenelm (1873-1965), the sixth earl, was a distinguished electrical engineer and president of the professional institute in 1927. He and his wife Lilian, a writer of books for children, restored the house to its original shape, wiping away the Victorian extensions. But their only son had been killed at Dunkirk and the title passed to a distant cousin, Edward (1903-82).

The Punch Room, Cotehele, contains superb
eighteenth century tapestries.

He was descended from Dick, the second baron; one of whose family had emigrated to New Zealand in the 1850s. Edward himself was a sheepfarmer there. He stayed at Mount Edgcumbe several times before he inherited the estate and title; Edward took on many of the local offices and played the same part in the life of Plymouth and Cornwall as the earls had done for so many generations.

His wife, always known as Effie, was a great support and took the lead in founding the Mount Edgcumbe Hospice at St Austell.

Cotehele had passed to the National Trust in 1947. Kenelm had inherited the estate at the age of 71, Edward at 62. Two sets of death duties in seventeen years, and the prospect of another set not far removed, induced Edward to make over the Mount Edgcumbe house and park to a joint consortium of Plymouth City Council and Cornwall County Council in 1971.

Robert, who succeeded as eighth earl at the age of 43, was another New Zealander and manager of a sheep farm there. Like Edward he lived in Mount Edgcumbe House for a few years, but then moved to a smaller house outside the park. So while there is still an Earl of Mount Edgcumbe in the neighbourhood he plays no part in public life; the old house, much restored, is open to the public and the park much enjoyed as a country park.

Mount Edgcumbe is now one of the few listed Grade I Historic Gardens in the west of England; its position with the sea lapping on three sides makes it unique. Its gardens which have been carefully restored are a monument to eighteenth-century taste, the product of generations of a family given both to public service and the arts.

— The Eliots —
Earls of St Germans

The Eliots are one of the rare Cornish families who, having made their money by trade and judicious marriages, bought up monastic land after the Dissolution.

They originated at East Coker in Somerset; T.S.Eliot the poet being descended from the original stock. A branch of the family was established in Ashburton in Devon by the end of the fourteenth century and an early member married the heiress of the leading business man in the town; 'the first of a long succession of heiresses that Eliots managed to secure as brides', to quote Charles Henderson.

John Eliot was established as a merchant in Plymouth by 1535, from whence he shipped his Ashburton corn to London. John was a partner with the renowned William Hawkins in town affairs, and mayor of Plymouth three times. He had made enough money by 1565 to buy the Augustinian priory of St Germans from the Champernownes for £500. There he created a dwelling house out of the old monastic buildings, and began establishing a park.

On his death the estate passed to his nephew Richard, and when he died in 1609 Richard's son, seventeen-year-old John (1592-1632) took possession, the most renowned Eliot of them all. He married the heiress of a rich Cornish yeoman, was MP for St Germans in 1614, and on his early travels in Europe met and made friends with the equally young George Villiers, later to become Charles II's favourite and Duke of Buckingham. John Eliot was knighted in 1618, and in 1619 was a witness at the execution of Walter Raleigh, an event which made him think seriously about his Stuart king.

Through his Villiers friendship he became Vice-Admiral of Devon in 1623 and set about his duties with great urgency, principally concerned to put down the pirates plaguing the coast. He managed to corner and arrest the most celebrated of them all, John Nutt in Torbay, only to find that Nutt had more friends at court than himself. In no time Nutt was free and Eliot in prison! But he went on with his work, hanging twenty pirates in a day after one capture.

John Eliot was in Plymouth in 1626-7 when the starving and near-naked army of Buckingham's came home from the fruitless raid on Cadiz. He was so convinced of his erstwhile friend's mismanagement of the affair that he impeached him in Parliament, only to find himself in prison for another eleven days. On release he continued to be critical of the government of Charles I, refusing to pay the forced loan of 1628. He was making the speech in Parliament when members held the Speaker in his chair until he had finished, and for this he was thrown into prison yet again. He was never released, dying in the Tower in 1632. John Eliot has been called a brilliant brain, but a zealot.

A modern view of Port Eliot.

Another John (1612-85) was MP for St Germans in the Short Parliament of 1640 but he took no part in the Civil War. But he was elected to Parliament on the Restoration, remaining an MP until 1678. His son David died in 1702, leaving the estate to his cousin Edward. This Eliot vastly enhanced the family fortunes, marrying an heiress of the Craggs, of the South Seas Company, while his brother married another rich Craggs girl. He organised the coup which brought the Parliamentary seats at Liskeard into the family as 'our property'. Edward became the member in 1722 but died in the same year. On his death Port Eliot passed to his son James. When he died in 1742 his father's brother, Richard followed.

Richard had been MP for the family seat of St Germans

when his brother died in 1722, but then moved to represent Liskeard. He was Receiver-General to the Duchy of Cornwall. But more important he was, like his neighbour Edgcumbe, an early patron of Joshua Reynolds. The family still owns a charming family group painted in 1746, with Richard seated on one side and his son Edward junior resplendent in red coat dominating the centre (see colour plates). Edward remained a friend of the painter all his life, and was a pallbearer at his funeral.

Edward junior (1727-1804) inherited at the age of 21, in 1748. He made the Grand Tour with his friend Philip Stanhope, the illegitimate son of Lord Chesterfield to whom the famous letters of advice were addressed, and lived as a elegant man of fashion in Georgian London. In

1754, after Eliot had given one of his Parliamentary seats at Liskeard to Stanhope, Chesterfield wrote to his son to tell him the news: 'This success... is in a great degree owing to Mr Eliot's friendship to us both... it was impossible to act with more zeal and friendship than Mr Eliot has acted in the whole affair'. No doubt Lord Chesterfield had paid the going price. Later on Edward was to give the seat to the historian Gibbon, a cousin of his heiress wife. Eliot was later to dismiss the historian from the seat and the two fell out, causing Eliot much unhappiness.

Edward junior was a great borough-monger of his day, succeeding Lord Falmouth and then Edgcumbe as the major Whig manager in the West. He himself was a Member of Parliament from 1748 until 1784; in his time he held the county seat and commanded seven borough seats. To be elected for one of his seats cost £1500 in 1750, but by 1780 the going rate to Eliot was £2000 to £3000. Not only were the family seats valuable: from 1751 Edward was Receiver-General to the Duchy of Cornwall, and from 1760 until 1776 a Commissioner for the Board of Trade of Plantations, both lucrative offices.

Port Eliot, an 1830 engraving.

With the changing politics of the century so the family support changed; Eliots were Tories under Queen Anne, Whigs with Walpole, Tories again with Lord North only to break with him over his conduct of the American War of Independence and to follow Pitt. Edward Eliot's reward was a peerage as Lord Eliot in 1784.

On receiving his peerage, Eliot retired to Port Eliot. There he began replanning his park, bringing in Repton to advise but not always following his advice, and in 1802 commissioning the architect John Soane to remodel the house. Edward was a man of taste and refinement, and apart from his friendship with Reynolds he was a member of the Literary Club, friendly with both Samuel Johnson and Boswell, who quotes him several times. Jeremy Bentham described Eliot as a modest, civil and good kind of man.

His eldest son, Edward James Eliot (1758-97) joined with William Mackworth Praed and Sir John Molesworth in founding a bank in Truro. He married a daughter of Wiliam Pitt, first Earl of Chatham, whom his father supported in politics. He died before his father and it was his younger brother, John (1761-1823), who succeeded.

John too was a banker, at first a partner in the London house of Biddulph, Cocks, Eliot and Praed. In 1892 he left the firm, and in 1803 was one of the founders of the renowned Fleet Street bank, Praed & Co. He completed the remodelling of Port Eliot, which his brother had started. John was created Earl of St Germans in November 1815, an honour which has been referred to as 'one of the Waterloo creations'. He may owe his elevation to his usefulness as a banker to the government during the war, but it is far more likely that it was his control of so many Parliamentary seats. On his death the title again passed to a brother, William (1767-1845).

The third earl, his son Edward Granville (1798-1877), was at first an active politician, but later a trusted courtier. He was elected for Liskeard in 1824, became a Lord of the Treasury and for a time was employed as a diplomat.

After the Reform Bill he became MP for the new seat of East Cornwall. In 1841 Peel made him Chief Secretary for Ireland, which office he resigned on succeeding to the earldom in 1845. He became Postmaster General and for three years he was Lord Lieutenant of Ireland, resigning in 1855 when Aberdeen's ministry fell.

From 1857 until 1866 he was Lord Steward of the Household and Queen Victoria's confidential adviser, especially on family matters. In 1860 he was sent with the nineteen-year-old Prince of Wales on his highly-successful tour of Canada and the United States. In Cornwall he was deputy lieutenant and Deputy Warden of the Stannaries; and was affectionately regarded as a good landlord.

His son William Gordon (1829-1881) who as Lord Eliot was Liberal MP for Devonport 1866-68, went to the House of Lords in 1870 by a special creation as Baron Eliot. His father did not die until 1877, so he only enjoyed the earldom for four years. A diplomat, he died unmarried, and the title went to his brother Henry Cornwallis (1835-1911). The sixth earl, his son John (1890-1922), was followed by his cousin Granville (1867-1942), who also died unmarried.

His brother Montague (1870-1960) followed his grandfather into royal service, and was attached to the households of five sovereigns, from Edward VII to Queen Elizabeth. His son, the ninth earl, Nicholas (1923-88), a major in the Duke of Cornwall's Light Infantry, saw service in the 1939-45 war in the Royal Armoured Corps. Married three times, he spent much of his latter years living in Tangier and then Switzerland.

Well before he died, Nicholas made over the house and park to his son Peregrine, the present and tenth earl who was born in 1941. He is a jazz enthusiast and for some years before his father died, Peregrine ran a pop festival in the grounds of Port Eliot, to the great displeasure of his

A family gathering in May 1964 to celebrate the family's 400th year at port Eliot; from left to right the 9th Earl of St Germans, his daughter Lady Frances Eliot, his heir Lord Eliot, his fiancée, the Hon. Miss Jacquetta Lamson, and the Earls's brother, the Hon. Robert Vere Eliot.

neighbours. He embellished the circular eighteenth-century music room by having a mural painted around its walls by the modern artist Robert Lenkiewicz. The painter, a highly unconventional character who owes much to Peregrine's patronage, is constantly setting Plymouth by the ears. In *Who's Who* Peregrine describes his recreations as 'mucking about'.

It is a far cry from the medieval priory which originally stood on the site and whose thirteenth-century undercroft is still under the mainly Georgian building. Port Eliot is one of the few houses that has not fallen into the hands of the National Trust and is only on special occasions open to visitors.

The Foxes
of Falmouth

The Fox family has been in Falmouth since 1762 as merchants and shipping agents. For two hundred years they have been in the same offices, a Georgian house in Arwenack Street, opposite the Custom House.

But how the family has spread in that time! Large families have followed large families. The genealogy fills nine columns in Burke's *Landed Gentry*. They have occupied at least seven country houses between Falmouth and the Helford River. Branches have been established in Plymouth and other westcountry towns.

The first Fox in Cornwall, Francis, was a relation of the Earls of Ilchester and came from Farley, near Salisbury. He married a Kekewich of Catchfrench near St Germans, and settled there. His second son, Edward, set up in business at Par as a general merchant. From this a business in Fowey developed, and in 1762 Edward's grandson, George Croker Fox, established a mercantile business in Falmouth.

It was an opportune time. Falmouth was booming as a port, stimulated by its packet service, its fine harbour and its position at the entrance to the Channel. It had become the biggest trading town in Cornwall, and in the hinterland the copper and tin mines were flourishing. The Foxes were Quakers, men of probity and honour, and like so many westcountry Quaker families excellent men of business. George's elder step-brother, Edward, settled at Wadebridge and from his children emerged the Fox firm of Wellington, bankers and textile manufacturers, and the Fox timber firm

at Plymouth. George's younger brother Joseph became a surgeon as did his three sons. One of them, another Joseph, was a founder and principal of the London Hospital.

Pilchards and tin were the major exports from Falmouth, with the port handling most of the pilchards sent out of the county. The new Fox company became heavily engaged in this trade, as well as with the growing import of timber. For over two hundred years the firm was to be important as timber merchants, operating four depots. Not until 1957 did the Falmouth timber firm of Fox Stanton merge into other groups.

From Falmouth to Redruth stretched a belt of copper mines, concentrated around Gwennap. The Foxes became increasingly involved in the mines towards the end of the century. The industry had been depressed by the short-lived competition of cheaper copper from Anglesey and the monopoly by Boulton & Paul of Birmingham of the supply of engines. In 1791 the Foxes lead a consortium which set up an iron foundry at Perranarworthal to make mining machinery; at one time it employed 400 people. They also built docks and warehouses at the head of the estuary and so created the now-vanished port. For forty years this dominated the supply trade to the Gwennap and United Downs mines, and the export of their ore.

Copper mining boomed. The Fox family in 1799 were the mainspring behind the revival of Dolcoath which by

The Fox office in Arwenack Street, Falmouth, a 1972 drawing by Philip Freeman. The large chimney on the right is the King's Pipe, formerly used for destroying contraband tobacco seized by Customs officers.

1850 had produced a million pounds worth of ore. All told the Cornish copper production in 1800-1850 was worth over £13 million, which the Fox family shared with ten other major families and smaller adventurers. The Foxes sold their interest in the Perran Foundry in the 1840s, and as the West Cornwall mines profitability declined again, under new competition from East Cornwall, so the Foxes pulled out of the industry.

George Croker Fox had two sons, another George Croker (1752-1807) of Grove Hill and Robert Were (1754-1818) of Bank House. Shipping was still the main interest of the partners, and in 1794 Robert Were was appointed American consul at Falmouth, with his patent signed by George Washington. This appointment continued for most of the next century, and at one time the firm represented thirty-six nations as consuls.

Its importance in the commercial life of Falmouth naturally led the firm into issuing promissory notes on their London agents as a means of paying bills in the early nineteenth century. They never, however, became public bankers issuing bank notes, even though George Croker's son, another George Croker (1785-1850) married Lucy Barclay, a great-granddaughter of the founder of Barclays Bank. His cousin, son of Robert Were and also called Robert Were Fox (1789-1877), married Lucy's sister Maria. As the firm's history remarks, 'the generations... spread over the region and started or became involved in many varied businesses. They used their connections within the family to great advantage, and being Quakers they married exclusively but judiciously within their own religous sect'.

They were also becoming country gentlemen with intellectual interests. Robert Were II bought Penjerrick, a charming house south of Falmouth and there began creating a wonderful garden for which he raised many hybrid rhododendrons. But his mind was concerned with mechanical and scientific problems. In 1812 he began experiments to improve the steam engine, and helped Trevithick, the great Cornish engineer, with various inventions. After his marriage in 1814 he made a honeymoon tour of Europe and formed friendships with Humboldt and other scientists.

On his return he began research into the internal temperature of the earth which his firm's mining connections facilitated. Robert Were Fox II was the first man to prove that temperature increased with depth underground. Then he began research into magnetism,

Robert Were Fox II, the scientist: founder with his brother of the Royal Cornwall Polytechnic Society.

and in 1831-2, with the aid of the Perran Foundry, made a new dipping magnetic needle of great delicacy. It was used by James Clarke Ross to find the south magnetic pole. In all he wrote fifty-two papers for scientific journals, and was made a Fellow of the Royal Society in 1848.

Robert Were's fourth son, Alfred (1794-1874), also a partner in the business, built a thatched house at Glendurgan and, when it burnt down, built the present house. He had already begun planting up the garden, in the 1820s and 1830s, designing both the walled garden and the curved drive. His descendants have continued to improve the gardens, set around a valley running down to the north shore of the Helford River. Today they are among the most famous gardens in Cornwall.

The seventh son of Robert Were I, Charles (1797-1878), also became a partner in the family firm and for over twenty years managed the foundry. He bought Trebah, close to Glendurgan, and created another still-famous garden running down to the Helford River. All the Fox gardens contained exotic and sub-tropical shrubs and trees, many of which were obtained from world travellers through their shipping interests.

Charles was also, with his brother Robert and others, a founder of the Royal Cornwall Polytechnic Society in 1833, and was several times president. He started the move which in 1842 led to the invention of the Cornish man-engine, which transported miners (rather dangerously) up and down the great depths which mines were reaching. Later he wrote a paper on boring machines in mines. He was also at times president of the Royal Geological Society of Cornwall and the Miners Association of Devon and Cornwall. But his deep interest was in Bible history, and he made journeys to Palestine, Egypt and Algiers in pursuit of his studies.

Not that business was neglected during the century. Shipping grew steadily, and in mid century forty to fifty ships arrived on most days. As copper and pilchards declined so the Foxes shifted their interests. In 1856 a dock company was formed with the family in the lead by 1863 construction was completed. The basic aim was to establish a repair base.

By 1878 shipbuilding had started. It has been an important part of Falmouth's economy every since, and the Fox family provided the chairmen of the company until the 1920s. In 1870 the partners started a towing company with some renowned tugs, and in 1872 they built their own signal station at the Lizard, to get the first possible information of arriving vessels. It eventually became the famous Lloyds Signal Station, and survived until replaced by radio after the First World War.

Robert Were Fox the second had three children. Anna Maria (1815-97) is said to have been the main inspiration behind the foundation of the Polytechic Society, and her lively mind made the most of the distinguished people whom she met through her father's intellectual interests. There were also world travellers and people coming to Falmouth for their health who were constant visitors, either to Rosehill where the family spent their winters, or Penjerrick. She never married, and on the death of her father she inherited Penjerrick, living there until her death. Five years after her death, Falmouth School of Art (still renowned) was founded and dedicated to her memory; it is now housed in Rosehill and the gardens around have been given by the family to the townsfolk as a park.

Caroline Fox, the diarist, at the age of twenty-seven. An etching by Herkomer after a drawing by Samuel Laurence.

Her younger sister Caroline (1819-71) is much better known because the diary she kept from 1835 onwards has been published, and is a source of delight to biographers of the period. People like John Stuart Mill, Carlyle, Tennyson, John Bright and even Cardinal Newman, were all friends. She travelled with her father when he exhibited his dipping needle at the Great Exhibition of 1851, and on her London visits extended her circle of distinguished friends. She too was never married. It is said that at the age of fourteen she invented the word 'Polytechnic' for her family's project.

Their brother, Robert Barclay Fox (1817-65), started his diary even earlier than Caroline, in 1832, but it is much less well known. The George Croker line died out in 1850 and Grove Hill was left to Robert Barclay. Robert had four sons and a daughter.

Alfred's line continued at Glendurgan, still playing their part in the family firm. His sons, Howard Fox (1836-1922) and George Henry Fox (1845-1931), were followed by George Henry's son, Cuthbert Lloyd Fox (1885-1972).

All these Foxes continued planting at Glendurgan. Cuthbert was Mayor of Falmouth in 1920, a county councillor from 1929 to 1947, and High Sheriff in 1946. All told the family has produced four High Sheriffs. Cuthbert's son Philip Hamilton and grandsons Charles and William have followed on in the firm.

As times have changed so has the business. The help for travellers the firm supplied in its early days has been replaced by a busy travel agency. The company has also developed a boatyard at Penryn for small yachts, and are also major suppliers locally of marine paints.

So the Fox family is still very much a business house, but the many members have never failed to play their part in local life, to support charities and sponsor developments. Glendurgan was given to the National Trust in 1962.

Glendurgan, seen through the gardens created by generations of Foxes.

Goldolphin of Goldolphin

As early as 1539 Leland was to write 'there are no greater Tynne Workes yn al Cornwal than be on Sir Wylliam Golacan's Ground'. His younger son Thomas, he wrote, had built himself a pretty house about four miles away, with a blowing house nearby. About this time the family changed its name to that of their estate, Godolphin (Godolghan, Carew called it), because the English had trouble with the original. But they had been established there possibly for centuries before, in Godolphin House, the earliest part of which dates back to the fifteenth century.

The house stands about four miles north-west of Helston, on the slopes of Godolphin Hill which has been described as a hill of tin. The family made an early fortune out of the metal, which raised them to the eminence they held in the county from Tudor to Georgian days. Leland's Sir William and his nephew Francis brought over German miners who taught new techniques, and in fact turned tinners who worked the surface ores into miners, who dug deep. They introduced stamps for crushing the ore, and by the end of Elizabethan times Godolphin mines employed three hundred men.

There were good times and bad, but between 1825 and 1843 Wheal Vor and its associated smelting house raised £250 000 from its tin.

John Godolphin was sheriff in 1504. His son Sir William (1490?-1570) was sheriff under Henry VIII, Edward VI and Elizabeth, and was five times Member of Parliament for the county. A good Protestant, he held no office under Mary. Basically he was a soldier, mentioned for his part in the Battle of the Spurs in 1513. He led a company of a hundred men against the Pilgrimage of Grace in 1539, and took a company of Cornish miners to the siege of Boulogne in 1544. They so successfully mined the town's defences that it surrendered. Two years later Godolphin was appointed Bailiff of Boulogne, and came home with a face badly scarred from all his wars. 'No less to the beautifying of his fame than the disfiguring of his face' wrote Carew.

In 1549 Sir William was sent to inspect the defences on the Isles of Scilly, along with John Killigrew. Killigrew was supposed to build a fort on St Mary's and spent a lot of money doing very little. So in 1570, the year that William's nephew Sir Francis succeeded his uncle at Godolphin, he took a lease of all the islands.

This Sir Francis (1535-1608) was a scholar rather than a soldier, a man of culture and reading who helped Richard Carew with his survey of the county. In fact he devoted his energies outside his study to the county and its industry, extending the family home with the profits from his mines. He was made captain of the fort on Scilly about 1580, and after constant warnings about the poor strength of the islands, was sent to improve the defences in 1590. By 1594 Star Castle, which still dominates Hugh Town on St Mary's, was completed.

He was back from the islands in 1595 when 200 Spaniards landed at Mousehole and burnt the village. Sir Francis, a deputy lieutenant of the county, raised a scratch force and marched agasinst them, but was forced to retreat

Star Castle above Hugh Town in the Isles of Scilly, built by Francis Godolphin
in 1590-4. The family leased all the islands from the Duchy from 1570 until 1831.

to Marazion and collect more men. Seeing the odds against them change the Spanish re-embarked and left. With the departure of Sir Richard Grenville from Cornwall, Sir Francis became the leading man in the county.

His eldest son, Sir William, was the first governor of Star Castle on the Isles of Scilly, and served in Ireland with Essex. He was knighted for his services but took no part in the Essex plotting. He was at the court of James I, and died in 1613.

Three of his sons, in spite of the family's Protestant leanings, remained true to the Stuarts in the Civil War. Sir Francis (1605-77) held the Isles of Scilly for the King throughout the war. When the young Prince of Wales was sent west for safety he stayed for a night with Clarendon and his council at Godolphin before taking refuge in Scilly. When it was decided to send the Prince to France, Godolphin went with him, and a few months later the Parliamentary forces occupied the islands.

*Sidney Godolphin, the poet killed in
a Civil War skirmish at Chagford.*

The great loss was Sidney (1610-43). MP for Helston, the family borough, at eighteen, he was the last Royalist member to speak in the Commons before the Civil War. Sidney was a poet at the court of Charles I and promptly joined the Cornish army at the start of the war. He was killed when only thirty-three in an accidental pre-dawn clash at Chagford. 'Little Sid', Suckling called him, and Clarendon wrote 'There was never so great a mind and spirit contained in so little room, so large an understanding and so unrestrained a fancy in so very small a body'. William the third brother, was colonel of a regiment which Francis had raised, but he was also killed in 1643.

A cousin of these Godolphins, John (1616-78) became a judge of Admiralty in the Commonwealth and wrote a number of books on law and divinity. His son William (1634-96) was a right hand man of Arlington, the post-Reformation politician, and an ambassador in Madrid. He went over to the Roman Catholic Church in the reign of James II and when recalled stayed on in Spain and died there.

Another Godolphin was at this time taking centre stage in the post-Reformation governments. This was Sidney (1645-1712), a son of Francis, taken as a page by Charles II in 1662, who was to become the first Earl of Godolphin. He rose enough in the king's favour to become Master of the Robes in 1678. Sidney was elected for Helston in 1668, and was First Lord of the Treasury by 1680. Pepys called him 'as wise and able a person as any prince in the world'. He became Baron Godolphin of Rialton in 1684 and the king said of him that 'he was never in the way, and never out of the way'.

Lord Godolphin continued in high office right through the reigns of James II, William III and Anne. He became a close ally of the Duke of Marlborough, and his son Francis married Marlborough's daughter. During all the Great Duke's campaigns, Godolphin was in charge of the Treasury. In fact the Duke would only embark on a campaign when he had Godolphin's support at home. But

Sir Francis returned to Cornwall after a short spell away. In 1650, after the execution of the King, Parliament grew alarmed at the possibility of revolt in Cornwall, and Godolphin along with other leaders was taken into precautionary custody. He lived quietly until the Restoration of Charles II, who as Prince of Wales had been well acquainted with Godolphin. The King made him a Knight of the Bath, restored him as Governor of Scilly, and gave him in reward the estate of Rialton, near Bodmin. Francis was lucky. Both his brothers died in the war.

*Sidney, first Earl of Goldolphin, Lord
High Treasurer in Marlborough's time.*

in childbirth. All his life he was a great admirer of the ladies, in spite of a perpetual gloomy expression. Godolphin never married again, but took his other compensations in horse racing and heavy gambling. When Queen Anne sacked him he was saved from real poverty by the death of his elder brother Sir William who left him £4000 a year and the estate. Yet in true eighteenth century style he had looked after his family; one brother Charles, MP for Helston, was the First Commissioner of Customs and his younger brother Henry (1646-1723) was Provost of Eton and briefly Dean of St Paul's. His son was made Lord Warden of the Stannaries at the age of 27. But Godolphin had worn himself out in public service; he was broken in health, and died aged 68 in 1712. Four dukes were pallbearers at his funeral in Westminster Abbey.

The second Earl of Godolphin, Francis (1678-1766), who married the Marlborough daughter, soon found that he had a domineeering and interfering mother-in-law, and a wife who was devoted to the poet William Congreve. They had two children but when a third was born during a long absence by him from the country, it was generally assumed to be Congreve's child. Francis Godolphin accepted this daughter Mary into the family without a murmur.

He took refuge from these domestic problems in his stables, for he was as devoted to horses as his father, and introduced into England the far-famed Godolphin Arab, from whom, with two other Arab stallions, are descended all the horses racing in the country today. Francis continued to look after the family borough of Helston, paying all the rates and taxes of his voters and even rebuilding the parish church when it was destroyed by lightning, at a cost of £6000. For a time he shared Penryn with the Bassets, but then gave up that interest on condition that Basset did not interfere in Helston.

His only son William, the thoroughly spoilt 'Willigo' of his grandmother Marlborough, who became Duchess of Marlborough in her own right, turned out to be a drunken

when Marlborough fell from grace with Queen Anne in 1710, so did Godolphin.

In spite of being at the sovereign's right hand for so long, and through such struggles, he has been described as an admirable head clerk when circumstances forced him to be a first minister. In the constant party struggles he was timid, cold and easily disheartened. Yet he was the principal minister in four reigns, was made a Knight of the Garter in 1704, Lord Lieutenant of Cornwall in 1705, and Earl of Godolphin in 1706.

He had married in 1675 a lady renowned for her purity in a court notorious for its lack of chastity, but his wife died waster and died unmarried before inheriting either title. The daughter Henrietta, who married the Duke of Newcastle, died in 1766 without issue, and Godolphin House and all the family interests passed to the third child Mary, who had married the Duke of Leeds. On her death in 1785 Godolphin passed to her son, the fifth Duke of Leeds.

Neither the last two Godolphins, nor the new owners, ever spent much time at Godolphin, and the sixth Duke of Leeds reduced the house in size in 1802. He was only interested in the Godolphin revenues and its political influence but began cutting that down when he found that Helston was costing him between £600 and £1000 a year. After the Napoleonic Wars the poverty of the Isles of Scilly became a national scandal, so in 1831 the Duke refused to renew its leasee.

In 1850 the family demolished much of Godolphin House, and the remainder was leased as a farmhouse. It was finally sold by the tenth Duke in 1921. Today only the name of the village of Leedstown, and its pub, the Duke of Leeds. remains as a reminder of the last chapter of the Godolphin story. Godolphin House has fallen into good hands; in 1937 Mr and Mrs Sidney Schofield bought it and spent much time and money in a fine restoration. Mrs Schofield still lives there and the Godolphin Trust she has set up received the Sandford Award for Heritage Education in 1993, the first time it had come to Cornwall.

'A Godolphin never wanted for wit', runs the old Cornish proverb, and with memories of the gallant young Cavalier dying of a Roundhead bullet in the porch of the Three Crowns at Chagford, we think of gay and amusing people. But that Cavalier was a serious, introspective man, and the great politician a dull, irritable man. If the true meaning of wit, that is intelligence and wisdom, is remembered, then it does fit so many of the Godolphins, from Tudor times onwards. Give the final word on this family to Hals, who was writing around 1700: 'such a race of famous, flourishing, learned, valiant, prudent men'.

The Gallant Grenvilles

In the great baroque gateway to the Royal Citadel on Plymouth Hoe are emblazoned the Grenville arms. In the south-western corner of this fortress is a stone carved with the legend 'Jo Earle of Bathe 1666', remembering John Grenville who was ennobled at the Restoration and made the first Governor of the Citadel. Ten miles north, Buckland Abbey was converted into a dwelling house by the Grenvilles and the hall with its panelling and plasterwork is as Sir Richard Grenville of the *Revenge* left it.

Yet of Stowe, their great mansion near Kilkhampton in north-east Cornwall, not a stone remains, only some humps in a field. In Bideford the site of their town house is unknown.

The Grenvilles came to the West before either the Arundells or the Courtenays, possibly with the Conqueror. Within a century they were overlords of Bideford and held land stretching across the Cornish border. Here they settled for the next 500 years. They were an ordinary landed family, serving as magistrates, marrying into local families, building up their estates, gaining wealth from Bideford's trade. A William Grenville was Archbishop of York 1304-15; their only distinction.

Lancastrian loyalty was rewarded after Bosworth Field when Thomas Grenville was made an Esquire of the Body to King Henry VII. He served as Sheriff of Cornwall, and made some appearances at Court, as at the wedding of Prince Arthur to Catherine of Aragon, when he was made a Knight of the Bath. After his death in 1513 a tomb of white limestone was raised to him in Bideford Church.

John, his second son, went into the church and held the living of Kilkhampton from 1524 until 1580. As he also held three other livings he was well off. He survived seven Bishops of Exeter and all the religious changes from Henry VII until Elizabeth, a real Cornish Vicar of Bray.

His daughter Honor married first a Basset and, on his death, Arthur Plantagenet, Lord Lisle, a bastard son of Edward IV, the last Yorkist king. He was made Lord Deputy of Calais but was neither efficient nor discreet, and was recalled under deep suspicion of plotting against the Lancastrian king. Imprisoned in the Tower, he died there within two years.

The foundation stone of Plymouth's Royal Citadel.

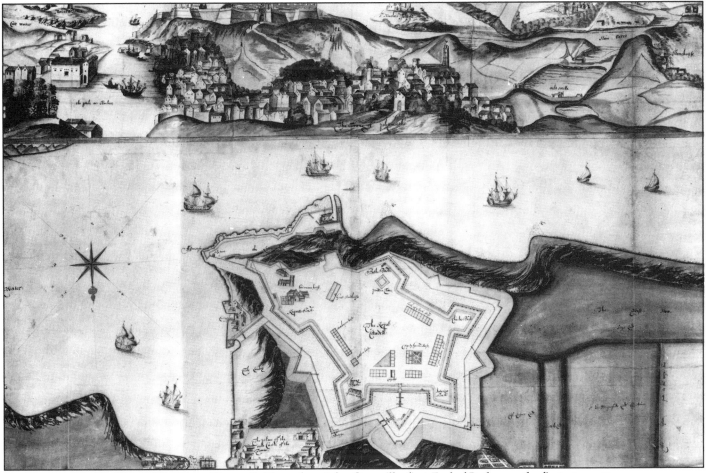

The Royal Citadel on Plymouth Hoe, where John Grenville, first Earl of Bath, was the first governor.
A drawing by Sir Bernard de Gomme, the engineer who built the Citadel.

Lady Lisle's elder brother Roger lived at Stowe from 1513 until 1523. He was three times Sheriff of Cornwall and attended Henry VIII at the Field of the Cloth of Gold.

Roger's son Richard was a bright young man about court, writing verse with the other blades of the day, Wyatt and Surrey. He was Sheriff of Devon in 1522, of Cornwall in 1526, Member of Parliament for the county in 1529 and with Piers Edgcumbe in the Parliament which carried through the breach with Rome. When his aunt, Lady Lisle, moved to Calais in 1533, Richard spent £400 and used his aunt's influence to get himself the lieutenancy of Calais.

When Lord Lisle was recalled in 1540, Richard stayed until summoned by the King with kind words. Monastic land was now up for grabs, and Sir Richard used his friendship with Secretary Cromwell to get his share. He had to pay, but in 1541 he bought Buckland Abbey, between Plymouth and Tavistock, for £233.3s.4d.

He played his part in local affairs, a JP for both counties, Sheriff of Cornwall again, buying up bits of church property. After Arundell, he was about the richest man in Cornwall. In 1546 he marched two hundred Devon men to Calais and led them in the French wars. In 1549, when the Cornish rebelled against the prayer book changes – to most of them English was as foreign a tongue as the familiar Latin services – the Protestant Sir Richard and Lady Grenville took refuge in Trematon Castle. But he was captured and flung into Launceston Gaol, never recovering from this ignominious handling. He died the next year, in 1550.

It seems that he intended Buckland Abbey as a home for his eldest son Roger, and had started converting the church itself into a house. Roger did live there, but in 1545 he was

Buckland Abbey, near Plymouth, where Sir Richard Grenville of the Revenge *completed the conversion of the church into a dwelling house.*

captain of the *Mary Rose*, flagship of the vice-admiral Sir George Carew, in the French wars. He went down with the ship off Spithead in that unexplained disaster. So on old Sir Richard's death all the estates passed to his grandson, another Richard.

This Richard (1541-95) became the most famous Grenville of all. In 1559 he was a student of the Inner Temple. Killing a man in a street brawl, he then became a soldier. He fought the Turks in Hungary, and then saw service in the cruellest of all conflicts, Ireland. Back in England he became an MP, and shared a famous privateer, the *Castle of Comfort*, with William Hawkins.

The western seamen were looking across the Atlantic to the New World, and Richard with his Irish colonising experience saw that the future there was not in raiding but in settlement. In 1574 he put up a plan to the Queen, with other westcountrymen, to find the southern route around America into the Pacific, and there create new colonies. But the Queen refused consent. Richard moved to Buckland where he had lived as a small boy, and completed building the great house, putting the date 1576 over the fireplace in the hall. Next year Francis Drake set off on the voyage Grenville had planned, around South America into the Pacific. On Drake's return in 1580 Grenville sold Buckland Abbey to him and for a time gave up American ambitions.

He was already heavily engaged in Cornish affairs. In 1577 he was sheriff and pushed his prosecution of the Cornish Catholics to new lengths. Richard captured the priest Cuthbert Mayne in the home of Francis Tregian. Mayne was duly executed at Launceston, Tregian imprisoned, and Tregian's uncle, the great Sir John Arundell, was gaoled for non-attendance at church. Richard Grenville was knighted in 1577 for this zeal in the Protestant cause, and continued energetically in county affairs, as JP and MP, for some years.

But in 1585 he went to sea for the first time. His cousin Walter Raleigh was now the prime mover in American

The Great Hall at Buckland Abbey.

colonising projects. In 1585, Raleigh being forbidden by the Queen to leave the court, sent Grenville out in command of a small fleet to settle a colony on Roanoke Island, off the coast of what is now North Carolina. On the way home he picked up a rich Spanish prize. Next year he led a support voyage to Roanoke, only to find that the colonists had already come home with Drake. So he left a second party of colonisers on the island. Again on the way home he raided and captured an island in the Azores.

Early in 1588 Grenville was ready to sail from Bideford again to Roanoke but, with invasion imminent, he took his five ships around to Plymouth to join Drake's fleet against the Armada. (The second party of colonists was never found again.). While the Armada threat lasted, Grenville was given command of the Cornish land defences. Later he was at sea with a small force guarding the North Devon coast. For the next two years he was in and out of Ireland, settling Munster (and acquiring land there).

In 1591 an English squadron was sent to the Azores to intercept the Spanish treasure fleet returning from the Indies. Lord Thomas Howard was in command, with Sir Richard Grenville as his vice-admiral, in Drake's Armada

The Revenge (centre) *engages the Spanish Armada rearguard.*

flagship, the *Revenge*. The rest of the story every Englishman knows, from Tennyson's famous ballad. A Spanish fleet caught them off Flores; Grenville failed to get away with Howard, and fought the famous fight 'of the one and the fifty-three'. Grenville was severely wounded, his ship a total wreck. He was carried to the Spanish flagship where a couple days later he died. *Revenge* sank, in a great storm.

Richard's second son, John, inherited his father's adventurous spirit. He commanded the *Virgin God Save Her* in the Armada battles, was a soldier in the Low Countries when his father died, went to Ireland to look after the family estates there, was at sea under Frobisher in 1593 and finally died in the course of Raleigh's expedition to Guiana in 1595.

The heir, Bernard, born in 1568 became the chief servant of the Crown in Cornwall. He was knighted in 1608 and became a devoted supporter of Charles I against his fellow-Cornishman John Eliot. He had two sons, Bevil the eldest and Richard, in whom the two sides of the Grenville character seem to be split.

Sir Bevil (1596-1643) was the good side. He began living at Stowe in 1625 on his marriage, repairing and rebuilding, planting trees, sending down pictures when he was in

London. Unlike his father he had supported Eliot against the King but could not stomach rebellion. He was the first to raise the Royal Standard in the West. Bevil had never been trained to arms but took to it naturally. He led the Cornish army to victory at Braddock Down and Stratton and then marched them out of the county towards Bath. He fell mortally wounded on Lansdowne Hill, universally mourned not least by his soldiers. All the memoirs show him as the perfect gentle knight.

His brother Sir Richard (1600-1658) is the reverse. Always a soldier, he saw service in the Palatinate and the Netherlands, was in Buckingham's expeditions to Cadiz and the Isle of Rhé, and commanded a regiment before La Rochelle. Then he was in Ireland, fighting the rebels. When he returned to London in 1643 he was feted by Parliament, and given command of a troop of horse against Basing House. These, with his back pay, he took straight to the King at Oxford. For evermore he was known as 'Skellum' (rascal) Grenville.

The King made him commander in the West with special regard to the siege of Plymouth. Buckland Abbey had been given him and he made it his headquarters, harrying the countryside with the utmost cruelty, even making some Parliamentary soldiers he captured hang one of their fellows. He quarrelled endlessly with his fellow commanders as he had with his wife, and was eventually dismissed his post. For everyone's peace he was allowed to get away to France, and there he died two years before the Restoration.

When Bevil fell mortally wounded from his horse at Lansdowne his sixteen-year-old son John (1628-1701) was hoisted into his father's saddle and continued to lead. He was knighted before Bristol soon after, and left for dead at the second Battle of Newbury in 1644. After the execution of the King, John found his way to the Isles of Scilly where for two years his privateering fleet preyed on Parliamentary shipping. Blake eventually captured the islands but Grenville was allowed to join Charles in France. Soon

he was back living quietly at Stowe.

John was in all the Cornish Royalist plots during the Commonwealth, worked with his cousin Monck for the restoration of Charles II and made the vital journey to France to tell the prince that the country awaited him. So after 1660 he was a great friend of the king's, being made

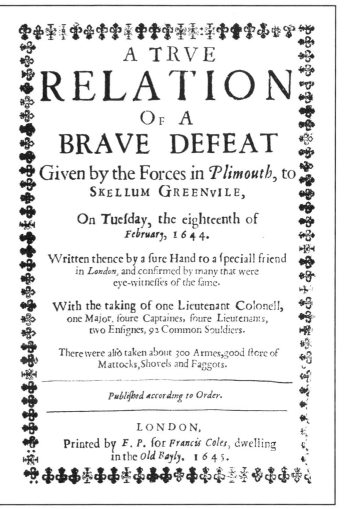

A Civil War tract relates the defeat of 'Skellum' Grenville.

Earl of Bath, given high office at court and in the West. He was both Lord Lieutenant of Cornwall, and Captain and Governor of Plymouth, presiding over the building of the Citadel. All these high offices brought him £3000 a year, enabling him to rebuild Stowe into a great classical brick building.

James II resented his determined Protestantism, stopped his grants and removed him from many offices. But he kept Plymouth and, when William of Orange's fleet came into Plymouth Sound, Grenville surrendered the Citadel. Again he became Lord Lieutenant of both Devon and Cornwall, But he wanted more, to be Duke of Albemarle, the title given to General Monck, on the death of Monck's son without heirs. William gave the title instead to his Dutch friend Keppel. John Grenville spent seven years in

The farmhouse at Stowe Barton, which stands on the site of the great Grenville mansion at Stowe, Kilkhampton.

lawsuits claiming it, and spent his fortune on this and on Stowe. He was described as a mean-minded man who only thought of making money, but he died in debt.

His son Charles (1661-1701), the second Earl of Bath, was a soldier who had served in the wars in both Austria and Hungary, and was in the army which in 1683 finally defeated the Turks outside Vienna. But he shot himself on discovering the state of the family affairs, and was buried on the same day as his father.

His son, William Henry the third Earl, was another soldier. He died in 1711 serving with Marlborough in Flanders. He left no sons, and Stowe went to the eldest daughter of the first earl, Lady Cartaret. She was made Countess Granville in her own right (John had changed the spelling in his claim of French ancestry). But she pulled down Stowe and sold all the material; there is hardly a great house in Cornwall without some part of the mansion.

The male line continued through Bernard, brother of the first Earl. Bernard's son George was MP for various westcountry seats before being made Lord Lansdowne in 1711. They went on playing their part in politics and serving as soldiers. His daughter was that Mrs Delany who turns up in so many Georgian diaries (Mount Edgcumbe had 'Mrs Delany's seat'). The female line produced Dukes of Buckingham. But the name has gone, and Grenvilles never again lived in Cornwall or played any part in her affairs.

A.L.Rowse sums them up: all Grenvilles, he wrote, had 'a harsh domineering note, proud in the extreme, unyielding, betraying signs of overstrain and unbalance, forceful, highly strung, bent on action, capable of the highest devotion; above all, exciting.'

The Piratical Killigrews

'For pyratts and rovers they have byn commonly knowen', was an early comment on the Killigrew family. Long settled beside the Fal estuary – indeed they created the town of Falmouth – they seem to have been a quick-tempered yet amusing race, indulging in various forms of lawlessness and always keeping good friends at Court to bail them out of trouble.

Their family crest of an eagle with two heads suggests a link with Richard Earl of Cornwall and King of the Holy Roman Empire. The family is first mentioned when Ralph Killigrew of St Erme, near Truro, was granted permission

Sir Thomas Killigrew.

in 1240 to bear arms. From here they graduated into trade in Penryn, and made enough money for Simon to aspire to marry the heiress of Arwenack in 1385 and so establish the family there. Though not large, the estate stretched from the site of the present Falmouth to the northern shore of the Helford river.

As early as 1447 Thomas Killigrew was suspected of piracy in conjunction with Henry Bodrugan, the leading Yorkist in Cornwall. He built up the family estates, some of which his son, also Thomas, lost when the Lancastrian Henry VII triumphed at Bosworth. But Thomas II remained a wealthy and leading figure in Penryn and in 1489, when bad weather forced the ambassador of Spain into the estuary for shelter, it was Thomas who entertained him. He had to enter into a bond of good behaviour when the Yorkist pretender Perkin Warbeck landed in west Cornwall to try and seize the throne, but otherwise prospered under the Tudors.

In 1546 a Spanish fleet put into the Fal, and there was attacked by French ships. Henry VIII decided to build forts at St Mawes and Pendennis to defend the harbour, and as Pendennis was on Arwenack land it was natural that John Killigrew was made its first captain on its completion in 1546. He was already engaged in privateering against the French and continued even when the war ended – which becomes piracy. John was concerned with the defences of Scilly in 1547, and became a county commissioner for enforcing the second prayer book of Edward VI, and to clear the churches of their plate.

Trouble came with the reign of the Catholic Mary Tudor. John's many sons were all in trouble. Henry, the fourth, supported Lady Jane Grey's pathetic ascent to the throne and fled abroad at the start of Mary's reign. John, Peter and Thomas were all involved in Wyatt's rebellion in 1555 against Mary's bethrothal to the King of Spain, and they too fled the country. They were at La Rochelle with French letters of marque, preying on Spanish shipping. Some prizes they sent into Scilly, but they were also working with their father, the captain of Pendennis, who in turn was in league with the pirates operating out of Helford. Both Johns, father and son, had spells in the Tower of London, and Peter in the Fleet prison.

John as a staunch Protestant did very well out of the Dissolution of the monasteries, and married a rich woman. But he had expensive tastes, and spent much money on rebuilding Arwenack into a house worthy of his grandeur. So he continued in piracy, and his association with the pirates based in the Helford river, to meet his expenses. He died just after his new house was finished, in 1567

His son, Sir John, inherited Arwenack, became governor of Pendennis and kept to his father's old ways. His brother Peter was provisioning the pirates in the Helford river and he and Thomas were still active with the French privateers. Two other brothers, Henry and William both took service at Queen Elizabeth's court, Henry as a diplomat and William as a groom of the chamber.

This John died in 1584, leaving an estate laden with debt

Falmouth: an 1816 engraving by W. Penaluna of the town which the Killigrews created.

to his son, another John. He too was governor of Pendennis but could never get Crown money for its support, and had none of his own. After the Spanish landing at Mousehole and the failure in 1597 of Raleigh's second attempt to destroy the Spanish fleet in Cadiz, he turned his attention to the Cornish defences. Raleigh expected Falmouth to be the Spanish target; Pendennis he found in a sad state and its governor no better. So Killigrew lost his command and went off to prison. He had never cut his links with the Helford pirates, and when the Spanish did land and attack Pendennis in 1597 he was suspected of having been bribed to turn over the castle to them. 'Was this', he asked bitterly, 'the reward for thirty years service at Court?' Even his house was partly burnt, to stop the Spanish using it against Pendennis.

On his death in 1605 another John succeeded to the impoverished estate. He took an idea of Raleigh's, and to the few fishermen's cottages outside the gates of Arwenack he first got permission to add inns, to serve the ships that were more and more anchoring off the village. In 1619 he built a lighthouse on the Lizard – the first in England, which in the end cost him far more than he ever made from it. In 1620, still with the aid of friends at Court - uncle William was still alive and in James's service now, and the Cecils were old family friends – he tried to get a customs collection and a market grant for his new town.

All this was done in the face of fierce opposition from Helston, Truro, and above all Penryn. Though the Killigrews over the years had married into the best Cornish houses they were not always tolerated by the major families, and thoroughly disliked by their neighbours, most of all by the people of Penryn. John did not prosper. His lighthouse cost money. Bribing officials at court for permissions to build his new town was expensive. His wife, who like other Killigrew wives before her was suspected of having launched murderous raids on innocent merchantmen anchored off Arwenack, fought him for ten years over a ruinous divorce case. A descendant wrote of her 'flagrant prostitution'. During the divorce fight she took refuge with the enemy Penryn, and gave the borough a silver cup in thanks for their support. Even the lighthouse had been opposed; the locals complained that 'it would take away God's grace from them, as they would have no more benefit from shipwreck'. John died in debt in 1633, and left no children to follow him. The only success in his life was to found the town of Falmouth.

On his death his widow, 'that old Jezebel Killigrew', came into Arwenack, and she was in possession throughout the Civil War. Not until 1648 did the true heir, John's brother Sir Peter, obtain the estate. He had been brought up at Court, 'a merry and desirable gentleman' who had built up a small fortune which he devoted to building up Falmouth. Within four years he had obtained customs facilities and a market for the town. By 1660, just before Sir Peter obtained the charter, the town had 500 inhabitants. It became a separate parish in 1663 and Peter built the church of Charles the Martyr, mainly at the expense of Charles II and his brother James. On his death in 1667 Peter was buried in his new church.

His son and heir, another Sir Peter (the family now had a baronetcy through an uncle) spent much of his time at court and was more given to 'speculative learning' than local management. When he did come back he found that Falmouth merchants had taken control of the town. Life was one long expensive battle with them. He built a new quay – now the Town Quay – and they fought him over that. His only son George was killed in a tavern brawl in Penryn. So in 1690 Sir Peter, once again with a mountain of debts, retired from Falmouth and died in Ludlow in 1704. The baronetcy died with him.

His younger daughter Anne had married Martin Lister, who managed the estate when his father-in-law retired. On her father's death Martin Lister added the name of Killigrew to his own. He built a granite obelisk in front of Arwenack House to preserve the family name, and gave to

Falmouth a town hall and a pair of maces. But he had no children; the estate passed to the two daughters of Sir Peter's elder daughter, and the main branch of Killigrews was at an end. The heirs did not reside at Falmouth, and the house fell into ruin behind Martin Lister Killigrew's monument. What remains of the estate had passed through three daughters to the Earls of Kimberley.

The Theatrical Killigrews

Old John, that first governor of Pendennis, had two sons who had sought their fortune at Court, Henry the diplomat and William, who founded the junior branch of the family at Hanworth in Middlesex. This William had served Queen Elizabeth as a groom of her privy chamber, and enjoyed her favour. A typical Killigrew, he maintained a large establishment in London and at Hanworth but he was always hopelessly in debt. He sat in Parliament for a succession of Cornish boroughs and continued to do so under James I, to whom he became Chamberlain of the Exchequer. He was knighted in 1603 by James, and his son Robert was also knighted a month or two later. Robert continued to look after the royal interests as an MP for various Cornish boroughs, where in various outbursts he displayed the Killigrew temper. He shared other Killigrew traits, getting himself in and out of prison, fighting duels and possessed of a wife 'a cunning old woman who... was too long versed in amours'. William died in 1622, Robert in 1633.

Robert's son William, born in 1606, was also knighted in 1626. He too sat for a succession of Cornish boroughs. William became governor of Pendennis in 1628 but was so ineffective that he was replaced in 1635. Still, he was close to King Charles II and was given command of a company of the King's Lifeguard on the outbreak of the Civil War. In that role he took part in Prince Rupert's great charge at Edgehill. When the first successes of the Cornish army had

fizzled out at Lansdowne and Bristol in 1642, Sir William was sent on a secret mission to rouse the Cornish gentlemen. They trusted him no more than they had his Arwenack cousins, and his attempts to get back the governorship of Pendennis upset them still more. He retired to Oxford, and on the Restoration again became a gentleman usher at Court, and vice-chamberlain to the Queen. In true Killigrew style he began upsetting his neighbours in Lincolnshire and began a new career as a playwright. He died in 1695. Two of his sons were soldiers.

William's younger brother, Thomas, is possibly the most renowned of all. As a boy he haunted the playhouses but being of a courtly family became a page to Charles I in 1633. He was soon writing plays; was imprisoned by Parliament in the Civil War but got out and made his way to Oxford. He joined Prince Charles in Paris in 1647 and on the Restoration became a gentleman usher at Court and vice-chamberlain to the Queen.

Thomas was still writing his plays, and in 1663 opened the first Drury Lane Theatre, which he built and largely owned. In 1673 he became Master of the Revels at Court, and was known as the king's jester; his wit often as obscene as his plays. 'A merry droll', Pepys called him, 'a gentleman of great esteem with the King who told us many merry stories'.

One son, Charles, inherited Drury Lane from his father and was in the royal households of Charles II, James II and William and Mary. He too was Master of the Revels in 1680. Another son, Thomas the Younger was also a playwright, and in the household of George II when he was Prince of Wales. The third son, Robert, became a brigadier general and was killed in Marlborough's wars in 1707.

Henry, another brother, also wrote a play but on the outbreak of the Civil War became a chaplain to the army, and was made a doctor of divinity. On the Restoration he became almoner to the Duke of York and Master of the

Savoy, in which office his 'improvidence and greed' led to the final ruin of the Savoy Hospital. His published work includes his one play, poems in Latin and a number of sermons. For the one parson in the family he runs true to style.

The sister of these bright sparks of the Stuart Court was Lady Shannon, a mistress of Charles I.

The Henry Killigrews

Henry Killigrew, the diplomat son of old John exiled in Mary's reign, served Elizabeth as a diplomat but was also a good musician and painter. His second son, also Henry, makes a final appearance on the Cornish stage. In 1642 he was a commissioner raising militia for the king; on the outbreak of war he was one of the Cornish gentlemen who joined Sir Bevil Grenville at Stowe, 'one of that rare company'. Though he never accepted high command, he fought right through the war from Braddock Down to Pendennis.

Pendennis was the last Royalist stronghold to surrender to Parliament, and gives a fitting end to the chequered careers of the Killigrews. As Fairfax and Cromwell made the final advance into Cornwall so the Royalists fell back until only Pendennis was left in their hands. When they were finally surrounded there they tried to set fire to Arwenack to stop it being used against them, but Parliamentary soldiers arrived in time to prevent its destruction. John Arundell of Trerice was in command, and Henry Killigrew a member of his council of war. From 11 April until 17 August the Royalists held out. When the garrison was allowed to march out with all honours of war they were one of the last in England to surrender.

Henry Killigrew was among them, 'quick of speech and resolute in temper, loved for his spirit and his sincerity'. He chose exile, but died at St Malo of a wound received in the siege, on his way to join the Prince of Wales. So, at the end of the story, the Killigrews were close to Arwenack: and they left heroically.

Arwennack was only partially restored. Today what survives has been converted into flats. It still has the appearance of a Tudor house, and sits very handsomely in pleasant gardens. On the hill above, Pendennis remained part of the country's defences until the last war, but the additions over the centuries have not touched its essential shape. Today it has been taken over by English Heritage who have installed old guns and furniture of all relevant periods, and have made a handsome presentation of the place. On the upper gun deck a reconstruction with dummy figures and reproduction artillery artefacts of the 1540s graphically shows local men practising with the guns.

Arwenack, the ancient home of the Killigrews
at Falmouth, today converted into flats and houses.
A 1971 drawing by Philip Freeman.

Molesworth St Aubyn
of Pencarrow

An Elizabethan lawyer who made a fortunate marriage, and whose heirs continued to do so; the familiar pattern is yet again followed by the Molesworth St Aubyns of Pencarrow. The family had been established in the East Midlands for centuries. One, Sir Walter de Molesworth, accompanied Prince Edward, later King Edward I, on his pilgrimage to the Holy Land and was Sheriff of Bedfordshire in 1297. From this family sprang the present-day Viscount Molesworths in the Irish peerage.

Seven generations separate Sir Walter from the first Molesworth to move to Cornwall, all of them serving their Midland communities. John Molesworth, a lawyer, was appointed Auditor of Cornwall by Elizabeth I, an office not without its rewards. He improved on them by marrying a daughter of John Hender of Bottreaux Castle. The castle has long disappeared, leaving only the harbour below its walls which now bears the corrupted name of Boscastle. John also bought the ancient estate of Pencarrow.

His younger son John was killed in 1627 in Buckingham's disastrous assault on the Isle of Rhé in support of the French Huguenots. His elder son, Hender (1597-1647), married Mary Sparke of Plymouth, the heiress of a wealthy Plymouth merchant who had served at sea with John Hawkins. For a century or so afterwards the Molesworths owned the Friary, just north of Sutton Harbour, and various parcels of Plymouth property, but

they let it all drift out of their hands. There was a Molesworth active on the Royalist side in the Civil War but the family seems to have kept the estate out of trouble in the Commonwealth. On the Restoration, Charles II knighted the eldest son of a second marriage, who had inherited the estate. This John (1635-1716) was Vice-Admiral of the North Shore of Cornwall, in which office he continued under James II and William III. John too married over the border into Devon families, first to a Slanning of Maristow and secondly to a Wise of Sydenham.

A younger brother, Hender, had settled in Jamaica where he became a member of the Council and then Governor in 1684. He supported William III when he ousted James II in 1688 and the following year was rewarded with a baronetcy. He died childless in the same year, and his title and his estates passed to the elder brother, John.

John's son, another John (1668-1733) and the third baronet, again crossed into Devon for a bride, Jane Arscott of Tetcott. This family, renowned in folksong and hunting legends, had become one of the wealthiest in the Devon squirearchy under Elizabeth and the marriage brought Tetcott into the Molesworth family. It is still used as a family home and Arscott has become a regular family name.

The fourth baronet, John (1705-66), was a great friend of Sir John St Aubyn, the Whig politician whom Walpole

Sir John Molesworth, the fourth baronet who begun building Pencarrow about 1760.

called the incorruptible little baronet. Sir John actually died at Pencarrow in 1744 and Sir John Molesworth replaced him in Parliament as a knight of the shire. He had married a daughter of Sir Nicholas Morice of Werrington.

About 1760 he began rebuilding Pencarrow into the gracious Palladian-style Georgian house we know today, 'one of the loveliest in Cornwall'. It was to be finished by his son John (1729-1775), the fifth baronet, who had taken

as his second wife a daughter of his father's friend, St Aubyn.

When his father died in 1766 he took over the county seat and remained in Parliament until his death. He was described as an honoured and enlightened Whig. In spite of this he had to battle to hold the seat, notably in 'the grand contested election' of 1774. The two Whigs, Sir John Molesworth and Sir William Lemon, the mining magnate, fought John Buller of Morval and Humphry Mackworth Praed, the Tories. The poll lasted six days. The Whigs won both seats, but it is rather odd finding Molesworth and Mackworth Praed fighting, because earlier on they had been partners, with Mr Eliot, in founding a bank in Truro. This bank was eventually to become Praeds of Fleet Street.

Sir John barely lived a year to enjoy his triumph, and was followed by his son William (1758-1798). William was the only son of John's first wife: his brother John was a son of the St Aubyn wife and John eventually married his cousin Catherine St Aubyn, co-heir of the fourth baronet.

Sir William, the sixth baronet, held the county seat in Parliament from his father's death until 1790. His son, Sir Arscott (1789-1823) took the title when he was only nine years old and he too died young, leaving his son, William Molesworth (1810-55) to inherit the baronetcy at the age of thirteen.

Sir William (1810-1855) was from youth a rebel against authority. After he was expelled from Cambridge he fought a duel with his former tutor. Travelling about Europe he became excited by ideas of Parliamentary reform and eventually became an MP for East Cornwall in the first Reform Election of 1832. In spite of what were regarded as 'infidel and radical opinions' he was again returned in 1835.

William Molesworth founded the *London Review* which became a platform for the extreme radical views of James Mill, long Molesworth's mentor. When Mill died in 1836 Molesworth bought up the *Westminster Review*, which James Mill had founded, amalgamated the two and made

Sir John Molesworth, the sixth baronet, and the third in succession to be a county MP for Cornwall.

James Mill's son, the even more renowned John Stuart Mill, the editor. It was the mouthpiece of the philosophical radicals. Among other things it attacked transportation, supported the views of Gibbon Wakefield on populating colonies and urged home rule for them. None of this endeared Molesworth to the Cornish Whigs, so in 1837 Molesworth found another Parliamentary seat, in Leeds.

Molesworth had pursued a number of ladies in his time, always meeting with rejection. He did not stand for Parliament in 1841, spending his time at home and in pursuit of the widow of Temple West. She had made her debut as a singer at Drury Lane in 1827 under the stage name of Andalusia Grant and married four years later. Sir William became her second husband in 1844.

The next year he was back in Parliament, but having again fallen out with his Cornish neighbours, stood for Southwark and held the borough until his death. On the formation of Lord Aberdeen's government in 1851 he joined the Cabinet as First Commissioner for Works. In July 1855 he was further advanced as Colonial Secretary, but died in October of that year. He left Pencarrow to his widow, the Drury Lane singer, who lived on until 1888, a well known member of London Society who was described as a resident of Eaton Place, Pencarrow and Tetcott.

Apart from left-wing politics and the ladies, Sir William's other great passion was for rhododendrons and unusual plants. As Commissioner for Works he was in charge of Kew Gardens at the time of the great botanical explorers, and his brother also sent plants and conifers from New Zealand. By the end of the century Pencarrow had specimens of all but ten conifers known to the western world. Between 1830 and 1840 he wrought many changes in the gardens of Pencarrow, and established the Italian and American gardens.

Sir William and Andalusia had no children, so the title passed to his cousin, the Rev Hugh Henry Molesworth (1818-62), rector of St Petroc Minor. This ninth baronet again died childless and his brother, the Rev Paul Molesworth (1821-89), vicar of Clapham, became the tenth baronet. The title passed to his son, Lewis William Molesworth (1853-1912). This baronet, the eleventh, was the first to live at Pencarrow for thirty-four years. He revived old family traditions, becoming High Sheriff in 1899 and being MP for Bodmin from 1900 to 1906. But he too died without children.

The heir was a great grandson of the fifth baronet, through that younger son who had married the St Aubyn co-heiress and whose children had added the suffix St Aubyn to their surname. So the twelfth baronet was the Rev Sir St Aubyn Hender Molesworth-St Aubyn (1833-1913). He was vicar of Collingham in Yorkshire.

Pencarrow, the Palladian-style Georgian house of the Molesworth St Aubyns

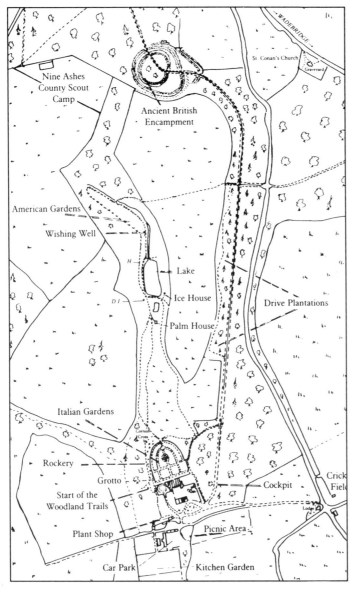

*Plan of the re-established gardens and woodland
walks created at Pencarrow*

His son, the thirteenth baronet, Sir Hugh Molesworth St Aubyn (1865-1942), played the old role of local landowner; appointed a JP Cornwall in 1903, on Cornwall County Council from 1910 to 1919, and High Sheriff in 1922. Although over military age he served as a captain in the county regiment at Bodmin from 1915 to 1919.

He too was followed by his son John (1899-1976), who lived at Tetcott before succeeding to Pencarrow, and so was a Devon magistrate before he joined the Cornish bench. He was chairman of Cornwall Agricultural Committee, and High Sheriff in 1948. Like his father, he was rather long in the tooth when the Second World War began, but served as a flight-lieutenant in the RAFVR. Old banking connections came up with his appointment as a local director of Lloyds Bank, which had absorbed Praeds.

His son, Sir Arscott Molesworth-St Aubyn, born in 1926, was a regular soldier, joining the Rifle Corps in 1946, serving in both Malaya and Borneo, and retiring in 1969 as a lieutenant-colonel. A Devon JP in 1971 while still at Tetcott, member of South-West Water Authority and Cornwall River Board, Deputy Lieutenant of Cornwall 1971; he served on a variety of bodies in Devon and Cornwall.

On inheriting Pencarrow in 1976 he found the gardens, which had been at their peak in the 1920s, a neglected wilderness. He and his wife set about re-establishing and replanting; Sir Arscott doing much of the work himself. He has a taste for new and unusual species, and has considerably enlarged the collections of rhododendrons, camellias and azaleas. Now there are 560 different species of rhododendrons alone.

Pencarrow is still privately owned, but the house and gardens are opened to the public during the spring and summer months.

Apart from the one Victorian eccentric the family has thrown up no national figures, but through the centuries has cared for the estate and served the local community from generation to generation.

RICHARD & HARRIOT ELIOT
and all their Children.
(with M.rs Goldsworthy)
(& the Hon.ble Capt.t John Hamilton)
A.D. 1746.

The Eliot family in 1746, a Reynolds' painting, with Richard Eliot and his wife sitting on the right of the group
but with their son and heir Edward, who was to become the first Lord Eliot, dominating the painting in his red coat.
The Eliots were early patrons of Joshua Reynolds, who was born just across the Tamar at Plympton. (Private collection).

Above: *Admiral George Edgcumbe, the first Earl, seen with Mount Edgcumbe park in the background. A Reynolds' portrait.*

Above right: *The admiral as a small boy with his big brother Richard, who grew up to be a member of Horace Walpole's Strawberry Hill set. A 1722 painting by Jonathan Richardson.*

Right: *The tomb at Morlaix of Sir Richard, the friend and supporter of King Henry VII. (All Mount Edgcumbe Country Park).*

*Sir William Molesworth, the 'radical aristocrat' whose extreme views upset the Cornish voters, and his wife Andalusia,
a young widow when he married her. She had made her name as a singer at Drury Lane. (Pencarrow).*

Sir Bevil Grenville, the leader of the Cornish armies in the Civil War. He had all the virtues. All the vices were in his brother 'Skellum'. (Peter Prideaux-Brune).

Sir Richard Grenville, the great Elizabethan who had both the bravery and the black qualities of the family. (National Portrait Gallery).

Kenelm, the Sixth Earl of Mount Edgcumbe with Lilian, his Countess, in their robes for the Coronation in 1953. (Mount Edgcumbe Country Park).

Richard, first Baron Robartes of Truro, described as 'the greatest money lender in Cornwall'. He had no love for the Stuarts after being forced by their government in 1625 to buy his peerage for £10 000, and his son fought for Parliament all through the Civil War. (National Trust, Cameracraft).

Sir John Eliot, painted just before he died in the Tower in 1632.
He had been sent there for his leadership of the House of Commons against the rule of King Charles I. (Private collection).

John Carew Pole, younger son of Sir Richard, in his uniform as a Page of Honour to the Queen Mother in 1990. In the Civil War one forebear was executed by Parliament and another was later executed for signing the death warrant of King Charles I. (Antony House, Robert Chapman).

Major General Sir Hussey Vivian (Royal Institution of Cornwall), *one of Wellington's cavalry commanders who led the last charge at Waterloo. All this splendour was intially paid for by the family's copper-smelting works at Swansea, which were run by his brother's family and later his nephew, who became Lord Swansea in 1893, seen here* (below) *in a 'Vanity Fair' cartoon.* (W. Fox-Smith).

Bishop Trelawny, by Kneller, wearing the robes of the Order of the Garter. He is the hero of the Cornish hymn, 'Shall Trelawny Die'. (Royal Institution of Cornwall).

The Bishop's grandson Edward, 'the Great Corsair', friend of Shelley, who fought alongside Byron in Greece: hence the Greek costume. He came home to be lionised in every drawing room. (Sir John Hawkins).

*St Michael's Mount,
home of the St Aubyns
since 1649. The family
fought for Parliament
in the Civil War and
bought St Michael's
Mount from the
impoverished Royalist
Bassets.*
(The National Trust,
Andrew Besley).

Place, Fowey home of the Treffrys since the thirteenth century. (W. Fox-Smith).

Cornwall's other Place, Prideaux Place at Padstow, which the Prideaux family built in 1592. (Peter Prideaux-Brune).

The Ship Inn at Fowey which was built as the Fowey home of the Rashleighs soon after they arrived in the town in 1529. (St Austell Brewery).

The Grenville Room at Prideaux Place, Padstow. The Prideaux family brought the dining room from the Grenville mansion at Stowe when that house was torn down, and moved it, panelling and contents, to Place. (Peter Prideaux-Brune).

Above left: *The pyramid memorial to the Killigrew family in front of what remains of the family house, Arwenack, at Falmouth. (Peter Gilson).*

Above Right: *Godolphin House, home of the Godolphins from the fifteenth century until their heirs, the Dukes of Leeds, sold up in 1921. (Mrs Schofield).*

Left: *A Georgian town house at Truro, built by Thomas Daniel in the 1750s from the fortune he made from the mines. (Western Morning News).*

A watercolour of Trelawne painted by Rose-Mary, wife of Sir William, the 10th Baronet, in 1868.
(Trelawny Collection).

*Trelawne today. The house is the centre of a
'holiday village' and the lawns serve as a children's
playground.* (Haven Leisure Ltd).

Pendennis Castle at Falmouth; John Killigrew was the first captain in 1546. The distant barrack blocks were added in later centuries. (English Heritage).

Falmouth Docks, started by the Fox family in 1856-63. (Western Morning News).

The ends of Cornwall; Trengwainton (above), *the most western of the great houses* (The National Trust) *and Mount Edgcumbe* (below) *the most eastern.* (Mount Edgcumbe Country Park).

St Michael's Mount seen in the distance from the terrace at Trengwainton; the colour in the garden gives a hint of the richness to be found in all Cornish gardens. (The National Trust, Murray King).

Trerice, the lovely little Elizabethan house built by John Arundell near Newquay, now a National Trust property.
(The National Trust, John Hicks).

The Prideaux of Padstow

The Prideaux are another family founded by a lawyer, but in this case one who took advantage of the opportunities afforded by the Dissolution of the Monasteries. Nicholas Prideaux, member of a widespread family of Devon lawyers, was in 1534 the 'man of affairs' to old Prior Vyvyan of Bodmin. He acted on the old man's dying wishes and did his best to have Thomas Mundy elected in his place. This Mundy was a son of a former Lord Mayor of London who was a friend of the all-powerful Thomas Cromwell, but in Cornwall the great Arundell had different ideas. He secured the election of his own man, but Cromwell was not to be beaten. In less than nine months the Arundell protégé was removed and Cromwell's man Mundy elected.

Mundy found himself highly unpopular with his neighbours and with Bodmin town; he also had other problems. The Dissolution of the Monasteries was already under way, and Bodmin's turn was coming. So Mundy started making favourable long leases of priory land to his family and friends; Prideaux his chief agent and bailiff rode to London to make sure it was all legal, and in the process obtained some useful leases for himself, including the great tithes of Padstow.

Nicholas Prideaux's brother Humphrey also had profitable dealings with the Prior, and Humphrey married his son William to a niece of Prior Mundy, and his daughter to a nephew. William Prideaux and his wife were granted a lease of the manor of Padstow. Then in 1545 Nicholas bought the freehold of Padstow, and as he was a bachelor and intended that nephew William should be his heir, everything worked out very nicely. William was succeeded by his son Nicholas, named after that benevolent great-uncle. Nicholas married an heiress who brought him the rich estate of St Breock, just west of Wadebridge and not far south of Padstow, and no doubt her dowry enabled him to build Place, the great house overlooking Padstow. Place was completed in 1592, a typical Elizabethan house built in the patriotic E-shape in the Queen's honour. But his wife gave him no children, and by 1593 his brother John had followed him at Padstow, to be followed in his turn by another younger brother Edmund (1606-1683).

If this branch of the Prideaux family was not particularly fruitful, other branches had so multiplied that by the Civil War they crop up everywhere, and on both sides. Edmund was for Parliament, but maintained his friendship with Bevil Grenville, the Royalist leader. He kept fairly quiet during the war years and most of the Commonwealth and only became politically active towards the end. In 1659 he was at Truro with other Cornish gentlemen, seeking a free Parliament, and was in constant correspondence with his brother-in-law, Sir William Morice, who was working assiduously for the Restoration of Charles II. He was in Richard Cromwell's first Parliament as MP for Saltash but he did not stand again. After the Restoration his influential brother-in-law secured a pardon for his Parliamentary stand during the war.

Edmund had three children, John, Edmund, a merchant of Smyrna in Turkey, and Humphrey, a considerable scholar and orientalist (odd that two sons should have

An 1830 engraving of Prideaux Place, showing the Gothic west facade contrasting with the Elizabethan south front.

been interested in the East). He was a doctor of divinity and became a distinguished Dean of Norwich.

Edmund was followed at Place by his eldest son John (1643-1704), Sheriff of Cornwall in 1699, who in turn was followed by his son Edmund (1672-1728). But he died childless and Place passed to yet another Edmund, son of the Dean of Norwich.

This Edmund(1687-1745) was a man of taste and no mean artist. Before he inherited Place he had visited many of the great houses of Cornwall and made pleasant pencil drawings of them – that in Antony library is dated 1727. He began improving Place, first removing the pointed Elizabethan gables from the entrance. He brought the house up-to-date internally, getting rid its old open fireplaces, and installing the new sash windows. He bought the dining room panelling from the Grenvilles' great house at Stowe, which was being pulled down at the time. This he used in Place, and the sitting room is still known as the Grenville Room.

Following the new romantic ideas of the day he made the Grand Tour of France and Italy in 1739, not as one fresh out of university but at the mature age of forty. In Italy he collected Roman antiques. At Place Edmund had already made formal gardens with hedged walks and an obelisk; now he added a classical temple, a grotto and an arbour

The Regency Gothic library at Prideaux Place, created by the first Prideaux to add the Brune suffix to the family name.

housing Roman souvenirs. He was a keen amateur in everything, drawing, architecture and landscape gardening.

His son, Humphrey (1719-1793), was another typical Georgian country gentleman, following his father's interests in the arts and gardening. He also made the Grand Tour, and preserved in the morning room is a pastel drawing of him by the Italian artist Rosalba Carriera. When the picture was cleaned in 1914 it was taken from its frame and behind was a letter from Rosalba declaring that she was in love with her subject. Whether this love was ever declared between them remains a romantic mystery. At any rate, Humphrey married twice, his second wife from Dorset being an heiress of the wealthy Brune family.

He was also an early patron of the 'Cornish Wonder', the artist John Opie born in 1761 a few miles away at St Agnes. In his teens Opie earned a living as an itinerant portrait painter, and Edmund paid him twenty guineas to paint all the family. In the morning-room at Place hangs a self-portrait by Opie, said to have been given as a tip to the housekeeper. No doubt she fed him well during his stay (in the servants' quarters?) while painting the pictures. The other Opie in the room, of Edmund's son Charles and his wife, must have been painted at a later date.

Humphrey shared his father's interests but not his father's views. He replaced the formal gardens with landscaping in the new style of Capability Brown, removed his father's obelisk and created the 'fortifications' across the lawn from the front of the house. Humphrey, who was Sheriff of Cornwall in 1750, kept up with the spirit of the times even in the place of his death, which came at Bath.

He was followed by his son, the Rev Charles (1760-1833), who had already added the name of Brune to Prideaux under the will of his maternal great-uncle. This first Prideaux-Brune was another true son of the eighteenth century, imbued with the Gothic ideas of Horace Walpole. He extended Place with a new facade facing west, a real Strawberry Hill piece which contrasts completely, and yet harmoniously, with the Elizabethan entrance front. He made considerable changes to the dining room, created a Regency hall, and above all a library of Regency Gothic with arched windows, stained glass and high fan-vaulted ceiling.

After these flamboyant Georgians come three worthy Victorians. Charles (1798-1875), High Sheriff in 1834, married a co-heiress of Glyn of Glyn, near Bodmin. His son, another Charles (1821-1907) was a Deputy Lieutenant of the county like his grandfather, High Sheriff in 1880 and a magistrate. The fourth Charles (1848-1936), again Deputy-Lieutenant, High Sheriff and JP, was a regular soldier, retiring as a lieutenant-colonel in the Rifle Brigade.

With a change of christian names came another change with Fulke Knatchbull Prideaux-Brune (1887-1939). The names come from his maternal grandfather, the first Lord Brabourne. Fulke was a captain in the Royal Navy (Emergency List) but also served in the First World War in the Australian Light Horse of the 6th Inniskilling Dragoons, when he was severely wounded.

His son John (1916-1988), born in Cairo to his father's Australian wife when his father was stationed there with the Navy, was converted to the Roman Catholic Church at the age of fifteen. He studied composition and the piano at the Royal College of Music and made a name for himself as a rather avant-garde composer. His Sonata for Violin and Piano was included in a London programme of the Society for the Promotion of New Music in 1952, and at the time of his death John was working on a composition based on the Padstow Mayday Festival, with its hobby horse and traditional song.

Declared unfit for military service in World War Two, he became an enthusiastic member of the Home Guard and was Welfare and Entertainments Officer for the Army in Cornwall. After the war John began restoring Place, which had been taken over by the American Army – an upstair bedroom still bears the legend 'Lance-Sergeants' on the door. A major undertaking was removing the false eighteenth-century ceiling inserted into the great chamber. This room, described as the crowning glory of the house, has a barrel-vaulted ceiling with the original sixteenth-century plasterwork telling the story of Susannah and the Elders.

The present Prideaux-Brune, Peter, was born in 1944. He is a barrister practising at the Criminal Bar, living in London in the winter and at Padstow in the summer. He and his wife have opened the house to the public and are enthusiastically continuing his father's work of restoration, both inside and out. They are rescuing long-buried formal gardens and employing artists to help them inside the house. Alec Cobbe for instance is producing painted panels with Cornish scenes framed in Gothic arches to revive the 1810 ideas of the Rev. Charles, who created this drawing room. The library is also being renovated. Nor is father's interest in music forgotten; regular concerts are held in the house. The 1991 programme included Nicholas Prideaux-Brune and the Downside Jazz Band – son and his school friends not quite on grandfather's wavelength.

The Brune estates in Dorset have gone to a cousin, but Peter still holds 3500 acres in Padstow and St Breock. The Prideaux-Brunes still flourish in the same place after four hundred years, and it is remarkable that in that time no title higher than that of knighthood has come their way – and that not since Stuart times.

Rashleighs of Menabilly

The Rashleighs made their fortune in two directions, firstly as merchants and secondly by buying up monastic land at the Dissolution. But having made a fortune in Elizabethan times, they lost it as a result of the Civil War and never became one of the major families of Cornwall.

Philip Rashleigh, the younger son of a successful Barnstaple merchant, began trading in Fowey in 1529. The Treffrys in their grand house at the northern end of the town had been there for two hundred years, and the Treffry of the time was a powerful figure in the county with friends at court. But Rashleigh managed to get some pickings from Tywardreath Priory in 1545, and Treffry was unlucky. Philip Rashleigh bought the manor of Trenant, on the Gribbin peninsula south-west of the town.

When he died in 1551 his eldest son had settled at Coombe, outside the town, but the younger son, John (1519-1582), remained in the town. He built himself a splendid town house, now the Ship Inn, where the date 1570 is carved in the chimney piece of what was the parlour. It is now a richly panelled bedroom. The Rashleighs became Fowey's leading merchants in the boom shipping years of Elizabeth. Even when in 1567 John bought Bodmin Priory, he preferred to stay close to the sea. Bodmin was let to tenants.

His son, another John (1552-1624), joined his father in the business. One of their ships sailed with Frobisher on his voyage to the Arctic, and John himself commanded the *Francis* in the fight against the Armada. By the end of the century the family owned so much property in and around Fowey that they controlled every election to Parliament for the next two centuries. They had at least two votes, sometimes three, to every one the Treffrys controlled. John himself sat in two Parliaments. He wanted his big house too, and started building a country mansion for himself on that monastic land out towards Gribbin Head. Menabilly is still in the family.

His eldest son, John, died in the same month as his father. The second son Jonathan (1591-1675) succeeded and finished building Menabilly. He was over fifty when the Civil War broke out, he and became an organiser for the king rather than a soldier. He lent money to pay for the first army raised in Cornwall, and was later one of those

Menabilly, the Rashleigh home where Daphne du Maurier lived and which she used as her model for Manderley, the setting of her novel Rebecca.

who collected and accounted for plate given for the Royalist cause.

He was with the king when Essex and the Parliamentary army occupied Fowey. When that army surrendered, Jonathan found Menabilly and his Fowey house looted, stripped bare and vandalised. He set his total losses at over £8000 and suffered still more in the Commonwealth, with a spell in prison and a fine of £1000 to get his estate

back. Jonathan lived to see the Restoration, and sat in two of Charles II's Parliaments.

It took the family a long time to recover from their losses. The family multiplied, supplying justices, sheriffs, and the occasional Member of Parliament for Fowey. Philip (1729-1811) sat for Fowey from 1765 until 1802, by which time he was Father of the House. He was deeply interested in Cornish mineralogy and built up a renowned collection which is now in the Museum of the Royal Institution of Cornwall at Truro. It is rivalled only by the collection of the British Geological Museum in London.

The Rashleighs sold their influence in the borough in 1815, whereupon the young Treffry heir threw himself into a strenuous battle for reform. Menabilly was entirely rebuilt in the early eighteenth century, and substantially altered a century later. In the middle of the last century the family moved to Point Neptune, above Readymoney Cove, on the Fowey side of the peninsula.

Among the twentieth century tenants at Menabilly were

A portrait by the Cornish artist John Opie of Philip Rashleigh, MP for Fowey for thirty-seven years from 1765 until 1802.

Daphne du Maurier in 1971.

General Sir Frederick Browning and his wife, the novelist Daphne du Maurier, who based Manderley in her famous novel *Rebecca* on the Rashleigh house.

Philip Stuart Rashleigh, born in 1924, inherited the estate from his uncle John Cosmo Stuart (1872-1961) and eventually was able to move back into Menabilly. He served with the Grenadier Guards in the Second World War and was severely wounded. He died leaving no children. His widow lived on for a few years but on her death Menabilly passed to the sixth baronet.

The Rashleigh Baronets

A younger branch of the family has also been prominent in Cornish life for the past two centuries. A great-great-grandson of the Civil War Jonathan became first commissioner and receiver for Greenwich Hospital. His son John Colman (1772-1847) was made a baronet in 1831. He bought Prideaux, a Rashleigh manor near Luxulyan, in 1806, and the next three baronets played quite a part in Cornish life.

Both the second Sir Colman (1819-1896) and the third, Sir Colman Battie (1846-1907), were honorary colonels of the

Charlestown, the harbour created by Charles Rashleigh, in the busy days of sailing ships.

Devon and Cornwall Miners Artillery, Deputy Lieutenants of the county and Deputy Wardens of the Stannaries. The fourth baronet, Sir Colman Battie Walpole (1873-1951), lived at Polmear, very close to Menabilly.

The fifth baronet was a nephew, Sir Harry, whose father had married a distant Rashleigh cousin from the Stoketon branch, from which Philip Stuart of Menabilly had also sprung. Sir Harry (1923-1984) served in the 1939-45 war and subsequently spent many years in Africa as an engineer. His heir, Sir Richard, born in 1958, is a businessman of some standing. He succeeded to Menabilly and moved there on the death of Philip's widow.

Charles Rashleigh

A younger branch of the Rashleighs settled in St Austell where they became successful merchants. Charles Rashleigh (1747-1823) grew rich with the development of tin mining and with the growth of St Austell from a village to a town. He built himself a fine house, now the White Hart Hotel, close to the church. He also built a suburb of St Austell, Mount Charles, to house the growing population.

Realising that St Austell needed a port, Rashleigh employed John Smeaton, designer of the third Eddystone lighthouse, to build a harbour, Charlestown, a mile or so from Mount Charles. The construction of the harbour took ten years and it was finally finished in 1801. Charles Rashleigh then built Duporth as a residence nearby. It is now part of a holiday camp.

The discovery of copper in the area in 1800 added to Charlestown's trade, and when the mines were worked out later in the century so Charlestown became important for the export of china clay, until eclipsed by Par.

Charles had no children to succeed him and he made unfortunate choices in the young men chosen to follow in his footsteps. This led to crippling law suits. Charlestown was sold and he died in relative poverty.

Agar Robartes
of Lanhydrock

Lord Robarts ... his great-grandfather was servant to a gentleman of this county, his hind. Afterwards lived in Truro, and traded in wood and fferzen [for smelting]: got an estate for 5 or £6000: his son was so bred and lived there too, put out his money and his debtors paid him in tin. He engrossed the sale of tin, grew to be worth many thousands [£300 000]. His son was squeezed by the court in King James his time of £20 000, so was made a baron and built the house at Lanhydrock, now the seat of this Lord Robarts.

So wrote a Royalist officer who was in the garrison at Lanhydrock during the Civil War, no friend of the Lord Robartes who was a general in the opposing Parliamentary army, a staunch Presbyterian and whose house the officer was occupying.

In the formal genealogical tables the first Robartes is Richard of Truro, in Henry VIII's time. It was his grandson Richard (1580-1634), sheriff in 1614, knight 1616, first Baron Robartes of Truro in 1625, who was squeezed by the court. In 1616, the year he was knighted, the Privy Seal extracted £12 000 from him under threat of prosecution for usury. Nine years later he was forced by Buckingham to buy his peerage for £10 000. He was described in 1613 as the greatest money-lender in Cornwall, and A.L.Rowse describes how the tin dealers would buy from the poor miners at £15 or £16 a thousandweight, and resell it to the

London pewterers at £28 to £30. Whatever his business practices, Robartes was a devout Presbyterian and clearly not enamoured of the Stuart court.

In 1620 Richard had bought Lanhydrock, that pleasantly situated estate in the Fowey valley, looking down to Restormel and Lostwithiel. It had been a posession of Bodmin Priory and after the Dissolution passed through several hands before Robartes bought it. He began to build a house there but it was not finished at the time of his death in 1634.

His son John (1604-1685), the second baron, inherited the estate, finished building the house and moved there from his Truro house in Boscawen Street. It was completed by 1642, the finest Jacobean house in Cornwall. John paid little attention to the new taste but followed the older English fashion with only simple embellishments. Originally the house had four wings, built around a courtyard. He built the gatehouse, linking it to the main building with flanking walls.

In the turbulent years leading up to the Civil War, John was the leader of the Cornish Parliamentary peers in the House of Lords. When war broke out in 1642 he promised £1000 to the Parliamentary cause, was sent by their Committee of Public Safety to the West as commander, and made Lord Lieutenant of Cornwall. But Cornwall was held by the Royalists and so Lord Robartes became a Colonel of Foot in the army of Essex. He fought at

Lanhydrock today.

Edgehill, and commanded a brigade at the First Battle of Newbury, charging in that battle with conspicuous courage.

It is said that Robartes urged Essex to make the disastrous march into Cornwall in the summer of 1644. Robartes came with him as Field Marshall, and the army established its headquarters at Lanhydrock. The king himself came down in pursuit, caught up with Essex at Lostwithiel and drove him back towards Fowey, trapping him between the river and the sea. Some 6000 Round-heads were taken prisoner, and Essex escaped by boat from Fowey to Plymouth, taking Robartes with him.

Essex left Robartes behind him in Plymouth in command; the town had been besieged since the start of the war. Clarendon describes Robartes as of a sour and surly nature but that the tenacity of his character made him well-fitted to defend the town. The naval commander there, Admiral Batten, wrote that the happy encouragement of Lord Robartes had roused the spirits of the inhabitants, so that they were resolved to stand it out to the last man.

The king himself launched attacks on the town without success, before moving off and leaving Sir Richard Grenville in command. The Robartes property in

The second Lord Robartes of the first dispensation, who was a stalwart for Parliament in the Civil War and commanded Plymouth in its long siege.

Cornwall, worth £1000 a year exclusive of the house and lands at Lanhydrock, was sequestered. His children were imprisoned; his plate taken and and sent to the Mint at Truro. 'Skellum' Grenville had occupied Lanhydrock as his headquarters; now he sat before the defences of Plymouth facing its owner. When Robartes caught a nephew of Grenville's in a spy plot he hanged him on the town walls in full view of the boy's uncle. Only the king prevented the furious Grenville from hanging three hundred prisoners in revenge. Grenville did not march away until the following spring, and Robartes was recalled to London soon after.

In 1648, with Parliament in control of the country, Robartes was appointed the county commissioner of the Cornish militia. But his Presbyterian beliefs, based on theology and deep reading in the library which is still in the house, was separating him from the Puritan fanatics trying to run the Parliamentary cause. He approved the Puritan simplicity in worship but did not want to separate from the Church of England. In 1650 he was suspected of dealing with the king, tucked away in Presbyterian Scotland, and for the rest of the Commonwealth took no part in public affairs.

John Robartes contented himself with developing the estate. He finished the gatehouse, which still bears his initials, and planted the avenue of sycamores which runs from the gatehouse to Respryn Bridge.

In 1660 he supported the Restoration of Charles II and in reward was made Lord Privy Seal and Deputy Lieutenant of Ireland. His son Robert (1633-82) was a leading figure at court, esteemed by the king 'for his lively parts and ready wit'. His daughter was a fashionable lady about town too, married first to the Earl of Drogheda and secondly to William Wycherley, the writer of the wittily-saucy Restoration plays. Lord Robartes remained active in politics and was briefly Lord Lieutenant of Ireland in 1669. In 1679 he became Lord President of the Council in place of Ashley Cooper, Earl of Shaftesbury, and was made Earl of

Radnor and Viscount Bodmin. The first title he chose, Earl of Falmouth, had to be changed when another peer was found to hold it. The story that it was changed when his wife was referred to as Lady Pennycomequick (the old name for Falmouth) is probably apocryphal.

His son Robert became Ambassador to Denmark 1679-80 but died soon after his return. When the Earl of Radnor died in 1685 therefore, he was succeeded by Robert's son Charles Bodville Robartes(1660-1723). Charles, the second earl was, like his father, friendly with figures in the fashionable world, notably Dean Swift the satirist. But he was also Lord Lieutenant of Cornwall and Lord Warden of the Stannaries. He died in 1723 leaving no children.

He was followed as third earl by Henry, son of his brother Russell, who had been sometime MP for Bodmin. But Henry cut no figure in the great world and died unmarried in Paris in 1740.

The title passed to John, son of his grandfather's brother Francis. This Francis had been MP for various Cornish boroughs since 1672 but his deep interests were in music, which he wrote in the then-popular French style, and science. He wrote papers on the similarity of notes played by the trumpet and stringed instruments, and became a Fellow of the Royal Society in 1673. John again led a quiet life in Radnor House at fashionable Twickenham, and died unmarried in 1758. With him the male line of Robartes finally petered out, and the Radnor earldom became extinct. The title was revived seven years later for the Pleydell-Bouverie family, Viscounts Folkestone.

John had not inherited Lanhydrock on the death of the third earl, Henry, in 1740 and the estate passed to Henry's sister Mary. Her husband, Thomas Hunt of Cheshire, had died the year before; Mary enjoyed Lanhydrock until her death in 1758 when the estate passed to her son George Hunt. He was MP for Bodmin six times, following his grandfather Russell. Neither the Robartes nor the Hunts seem to have indulged in the borough-mongering of so many Cornish families, but were content with their own

fiefdom of Bodmin, virtually on the northern borders of their land.

George Hunt was a rich man with extensive estates and a considerable income from the family's tin-mining interests in West Cornwall; the mining links that go back to the founder of the family never failed. At Lanhydrock

Thomas James Agar, for twenty-one years MP for Bodmin, became the first Lord Robartes of the second dispensation and added the Robartes suffix to his surname.

Lanhydrock in the great fire of 1881.

George Hunt pulled down the east wing of the house to establish its present form, and removed the walls linking it to the gatehouse. He added a double row of beech trees to each side of the sycamore avenue to Respryn Bridge, and created the present wooded landscape. He was a considerable philanthropist as well as an MP, but he never married.

When he died in 1798 the estate passed to his niece Anna (1771-1861), who had married Charles Agar (1769-1811).

The Agars were a Yorkshire family which had settled in Ireland in the seventeenth century. Charles's father served in Parliament for many years and held minor government offices; as reward he became the first Viscount Clifden in 1781.

The son of Anna and Charles Agar, Thomas James (1808-82), added the surname Robartes to the Agar in 1822. The Bodmin borough had disappeared under the Reform Act of 1832 but family influences did not fade and T.J.Agar-

Robartes was MP for East Cornwall (the new enlarged constituency) from 1847 to 1868. Maintaining the radical tradition of the family he remained faithful to the Whig sucessors, the Liberals. When he retired from the House this first Agar-Robartes was made Lord Robartes.

The mines were booming. Wheal Agar and the East Pool & Agar were among the rich seams around Redruth. East Pool was still the richest mine as late as 1918, when so many others were exhausted. Lord Robartes was a good landlord both on the estate and in the mining areas, and built and maintained the Miner's Infirmary at Redruth. He was a leader of the movement to carve the Diocese of Truro from Exeter, and became a major contributor to the cost of building Truro Cathedral.

In 1857 Giles Gilbert Scott was employed to enlarge Lanhydrock house and remodel the interior. He linked the house with the gatehouse again with low walls, and laid out formal gardens. Then, in 1881, the house was burnt down, all but the north wing and entrance porch. Lady Robartes was brought down from her window by ladder, but the shock was too much; she died a few days later and Lord Robartes died the next year.

Their son Thomas (1844-1930), elected for East Cornwall in 1880, became the second Lord Robartes. He rebuilt the house and lived there quietly with his nine children. In 1899 he inherited the Agar title as the fifth Viscount Clifden.

His eldest son, another Thomas , MP for East Cornwall and then St Austell, the very popular Tommy, was a major in the Coldstream Guards and died of wounds received at the Battle of Loos in 1915. So the title passed in 1930 to his next brother Gerald, seventh Viscount Clifden (1885-1966). He served in the Diplomatic Corps from 1906 until 1927, was on the Council of the Duchy of Cornwall 1939-52, and a Lord-in-Waiting to King George VI during the war years.

He lived quietly at home at Lanhydrock after the war, modernising the gardens with now-mature magnolias. He was a bachelor, living with his two unmarried sisters Everilda and Violet. They gave the house and park to the National Trust in 1953 but the three continued to live there. Elverilda, who died in 1969, was the last Robartes to live at Lanhydrock.

The title had passed to another brother, Arthur (1887-1974). A major in the Grenadier Guards in the First World War, he was wounded three times. After the war he went into the City until he retired to Jersey. He too never married and with him the Clifden title became extinct.

If members of the family were remarkable in the early days for their zeal in the Parliamentary cause, they were equally distinguished in the nineteenth and twentieth centuries as the leading Liberals in the county. In their latter days at Lanhydrock the last viscount and his two sisters, all unmarried, giving their time and money to good works, living together into their seventies, were regarded as old-fashioned survivors of an earlier age.

The last Lord Clifden with his sisters Violet and Everilda, on holiday in Brussels in the 1920s.

St Aubyns of Clowance and the Mount

The St Aubyns, called 'this gentle and knightly family' by Hals, came from Brittany, the first being a soldier in William the Conqueror's invading army. They were settled in Somerset until Guy in the mid fourteenth century married the heiress of Colquite, near St Mabyn, and moved west. He was knighted by Richard II, and served his turn as Sheriff of Cornwall.

His son Geoffrey followed father's footsteps and married another heiress, Elizabeth Kimyel of Clowance, between Camborne and Helston. Here his son, another Geoffrey, settled. The family continued marrying into other landed families, taking their turns as sheriff, and living the life of the minor Cornish gentry.

Thomas, in the days of Henry VIII, married a sister of Lady Lisle and managed her estate at Tehidy when she was at Calais, where her husband was Lord Deputy. His reports to her are amusing: A.L.Rowse calls him 'a merry, facetious character' and his wife wrote that 'youth had ruled him before but now he is well amended'. Their son John was a partner in a tin mine with Carsnew, the Elizabethan diarist.

It was his grandson, John, who first played a more prominent part in Cornish affairs. He declared for Parliament at the onset of the Civil War and served in the Plymouth garrison during the siege of the town as a colonel of horse (his brother Thomas was a colonel in the Royalist army). In 1647 John was appointed Captain of

Mount St Michael. He earned the thanks of Parliament for his part in putting down a Royalist uprising in Cornwall in 1648, and in that year bought the Mount from Sir Arthur Basset. St Aubyn continued to maintain a garrison on the Mount until ordered to disband it by General Monck, the last garrison of the war to be stood down.

Like all the moderate Parliamentarians of the West, he welcomed the return of Charles II, and set up the royal coat of arms in the Chevy Chase Room of the Mount in 1660, to celebrate the Restoration. He continued as Vice-Admiral of the county, serving in one or two Parliaments. He remained at Clowance, that pleasant house overlooking the lake in the parish of Crowan. It is not far from the Mount, and legend has it that he actually died in 1684 crossing the causeway to the Mount.

His eldest son, John (1645-1699), was made a baronet for his military service in Ulster. His son John (1670-1714), the second baronet, spent much time on the Mount in solitary retirement.

The third baronet, John (1699-1744) was a quiet man as well, insofar as his Parliamentary performance is concerned. He was fifteen when he inherited the baronetcy, and twenty-two when he entered Parliament as an MP for Cornwall. (The two county members, the 'knights of the shire', were always regarded as of more importance than mere borough members, certainly in the eighteenth century when borough seats were bought and sold.). He remained an MP for Cornwall until his death in 1744, but he spoke very little in the House. When he did speak it was with authority, and was heard with respect.

These were the years of Walpole's domination and the Prime Minister expected to buy men with offers of seats and, once they were in Parliament, with office. But Sir John St Aubyn consistently opposed Walpole. He once refused the Admiralty and Walpole in exasperation remarked of his fellow MPs, 'All these men have their price, except the little Cornish baronet'. By the early 1740s Walpole's long run in office was under pressure, and St

Sir John St Aubyn, MP for Cornwall in Walpole's time, 'the incorruptible little baronet'. This painting hangs at Pencarrow, a reminder of his great friendship with the Molesworths.

Aubyn was the mover of a motion demanding an inquiry into the last twenty years of government. This was defeated the first time, carried the second time, and St Aubyn was invited to chair the inquiry. But he refused.

Sir John had married a co-heiress of Sir Nicholas Morice, descended from the Morice who was Charles II's Secretary of State on the Restoration. When Sir Nicholas died he left £10 000 in cash to his daughter – the money was transported in two carts nearly the whole length of Cornwall, from Werrington to Clowance, all in half-crowns! More important he also left to the St Aubyns the manor of Stoke Damerel, near Plymouth.

In this manor was the new dockyard which William III in 1690 had built on land leased from Morice. As the town of Plymouth Dock, which in time became Devonport, grew up around the new dockyard, so the careful Morices and after them the St Aubyns only allowed the houses to be built on leasehold land. Not until 1857 did the Crown finally escape this strait-jacket, but the St Aubyn estate continued its three-lives leases with no renewal on its other properties. Even by the end of the eighteenth century the manor was providing a rent roll of £6000 a year.

Sir John was a friend both of Pope and the Cornish antiquarian William Borlase, who served for a time as tutor to his son. While Borlase was sending up mineral specimens to decorate Pope's grotto at his Gothic villa at Twickenham, St Aubyn (whose London house was in Golden Square) began to develop the romantic priory on St Michael's Mount in the same Gothic taste. He converted the ruined Lady Chapel into the present blue drawing room, and bought Chippendale chairs to match. He also had an eye to business; for in 1727 he had rebuilt the little harbour at the Mount to facilitate the export of copper and tin. He died in 1744, before the refurnishing of the house was finished, but his son completed the work.

This Sir John (1726-1772), the fourth baronet, was still at Oxford when his father died, and was much cared for by his Molesworth and Morice relations. He still lived like his

Fore Street, Devonport, in 1832, looking towards the Dockyard gates. The St Aubyn family owned the manor and for centuries only permitted building on leasehold.

father at Clowance but continued his father's work of repairing and restoring the Mount. He had the family barge built and designed the uniform for the crew: barge and uniform are still on parade for major events. He sat for eleven years in Parliament.

His son, yet another John (1758-1839), was only fourteen when he became the fifth baronet. Before he left Westminster School he was in trouble over money, and his expensive tastes never left him. He showed his appreciation of the arts by his patronage of John Opie, the Cornish painter, and was the archetypal man of the age, elected both to the Society of Antiquaries of London and

The St Michael's Mount barge crew, in the eighteenth-century uniform which is still worn on ceremonial occasions.

the Royal Society. He made a renowned collection of minerals (which he later presented to Devonport), and on his death an auction of his etchings and engravings lasted for seventeen days.

An early liason with Juliana Vinnicombe, a girl from Marazion (on the mainland opposite St Michael's Mount) was not blessed by marriage until 1822, by which time she had borne him fifteen children.

But he did not neglect his public duties, being sheriff in 1781, and an MP for various Cornish boroughs from 1784 until 1812. He sat as a Whig, being helped considerably in politics by his cousin Francis Basset, later Lord Dunstanville. Sir John was also Provincial Grand Master of the Cornish freemasons from 1785 until his death in 1839.

St Aubyn took care to develop his properties, and encouraged the commercial and fishing development of St Michael's Mount harbour, which he improved. Where there was one house on the Mount in 1700, there were fifty-three by 1811. When a French frigate drove aground on the island in the Napoleonic wars (it was the last time shots were fired from the fort), Sir John took its guns with their Republican badges and dates, and set them up on the Mount (the last two were stolen in 1985). He restored the church in 1811, and put the glass into the rose window.

St Aubyn also made the most of his growing town of Plymouth Dock. With George Edgcumbe he built Stonehouse Bridge, linking Devonport with Stonehouse and Plymouth, in 1772. By the end of the century the tolls were paying them £2000 a year. As Edgcumbe developed Stonehouse, so St Aubyn encouraged the growth of Devonport, which early in the nineteenth century exceeded Plymouth in population and swelled his rent roll. He resented the competition which Pole Carew started across the river with his development of Torpoint, and did his best to upset the ferry which Pole Carew and Lord Edgcumbe launched – but within a few years joined the partnership. When Plymouth Dock planned a grandiose town hall he gave the land, and on its completion gave two large Opie paintings from his great collection in the Mount. He supported its change of name to Devonport, and when it became a borough presented a Corporation mace.

He died in 1839 at the ripe old age of eighty-one at Lime Grove, Putney, a few miles down the Thames from Twickenham where Pope and Walpole's son Horace had their villas. His body was taken to Cornwall for burial, lying in state at Devonport on the way with full Corporation honours. There was more lying in state at Truro, which he had represented in Parliament, and at Clowance. He was buried at Crowan with full masonic honours, and an estimated twenty to thirty thousand followed his cortège.

Clowance and the entailed estates passed to his nephew, the Rev John Molesworth of Crowan. The Mount and the Devonport estate went to his eldest natural son James but it was laden with debts of £130 000. The fifth baronet had spent most that money on providing marriage portions for thirteen of his bastard children. Seven years after his death Queen Victoria and Prince Albert visited St Michael's Mount but there was no St Aubyn there to greet them because of the remaining weight of debt. But the Queen's footprints were recorded on the landing steps, and the Prince Consort played the organ.

James's younger brother Edward (1799-1872) played a major part in Devonport's fight for incorporation as a borough, and became its first mayor in 1837. He presented the new borough with a gold mayoral chain which he wore again in 1849, and which is still in the Plymouth regalia. As the century wore on the leasehold system and the rigid control it imposed on development grew more and more hated. Slum clearance and street widening was delayed until forced by popular protest and moral outrage. The freehold system slowly came into operation. The manor now has very little property in the town, and no influence.

Edward inherited the Mount on his brother's death in 1862 and in 1866 Mr Gladstone restored the lapsed baronetcy. By this time his eldest son John (1829-1908) was already a respected figure in the county. He had been a county MP since 1858 as a Liberal, and continued in the seat until county seats disappeared in 1885. Then he became the Liberal-Unionist MP for St Ives. He retired from the Commons in 1887 when he was raised to the peerage by Lord Salisbury as Lord St Levan. Devonport saluted the new peer by electing him their mayor in two years, 1890 and 92. In the five years after inheriting the Mount he built the Victorian east wing, designed by his architect cousin Piers St Aubyn.

His eldest son John (1857-1940) was a regular soldier, as was his brother Edward. John distinguished himself in the Sudan and the Nile Expedition, and was military secretary to the Governor-General of Canada 1892-4. When he became the second baron on his father's death in 1908 he had been commanding the Grenadier Guards since 1904. Edward his brother served in Egypt and South Africa, and was on active service in the First World War when he was drowned, aboard HMS *Persia* in 1915.

This second Lord St Levan was a Deputy Lieutenant for the county and Deputy Warden of the Stannaries. He rejoined the Army in 1916 at the age of 59 and became

The fourth Lord St Levan, seated in the Chevy Chase Room at St Michael's Mount.

brigadier-general commanding the Reserve Western Division Territorial Army. It was this soldier who collected pictures for the gallery on the Mount, and rare plants and shrubs for the garden. He created too a shelter-belt of trees on the island.

On his death the title and the Mount passed to his nephew Francis (1895-1978), another soldier. He too was a major in the Grenadier Guards on his succession, and saw service in both world wars. He retired as a regular solider in 1941 and became colonel commandant of the West Cornwall Home Guard. During this time war came again to the island, for a platoon of infantry was stationed there in the early days of the Second World War, and anti-invasion blockhouses erected on its shores. It was once machine-gunned by German aircraft. In 1950 the battleship *Warspite*, on its way to the breakers yard, was stranded and eventually broken up on the beach beside the Mount.

In 1956 the island and house were made over to the National Trust, although the Victorian wing built by the first baron was leased back to the family and has been their home ever since.

The fourth Lord St Levan, John, born in 1919, won the Distinguished Service Cross as a lieutenant in the Royal Naval Volunteer Reserve in 1944. He has played his part in county affairs, being a Deputy-Lieutenant since 1977 and sheriff in 1978. He became a fellow of the Royal Society of Arts in 1974, the year in which he published an admirable history of St Michael's Mount. Lord St Levan has been president of the Friends of Plymouth Art Gallery since 1985, and is a past-president of the Cornwall Council for the Protection of Rural England, and of the Royal Bath and West of England Society.

Lord St Levan has no children but his brother, the Hon. Piers St Aubyn, has two sons James and Nicholas, and they in turn have both two sons. So the family, which has so long a history and has been through various vissicitudes, should long flourish.

Treffrys of Fowey

'The glory of Fowey' was Leland's description of Place, the house where the Treffrys have lived for over six hundred years. A 'fair and ancient house, castle-wise builded... overlooketh the town and haven with a pleasant prospect', wrote Carew in his *Survey of Cornwall*. The Treffrys owed their original fortunes to trading out of the port in the great days of the 'Gallants of Fowey', and by their support for the Tudors.

The family is descended from Roger Treffry of Treffry in Lanhydrock. His great-great-grandson Thomas married an heiress who brought the manor of Fowey and Place into the family. His grandson John fought at Crecy and then at Poitiers in 1356, where he was knighted by the Black Prince for capturing the French royal standard.

In the lawless years of the Wars of the Roses the sea captains and merchants of Fowey prospered, partly by piracy and intimidating their rivals. They even fought a pitched battle with men of the Cinque Ports, and beat them. The Treffrys took their share of this trading, and in 1433 Thomas Treffry, a great-grandson of Sir John of Poitiers, became havener for Plymouth and Cornwall. On top of this important and lucrative office he also married an heiress. The Treffrys were growing rich.

His son, another Thomas, was also havener for Fowey and became a gentleman usher to King Henry VI. In these days the seamen of the West of England made regular raids on the Breton and Norman ports across the Channel, and equally regularly the Frenchmen replied. While Thomas was away on court duties in 1457 the French raided Fowey, swept through the town and attacked Place itself. With great courage his wife Elizabeth defended her home, pouring boiling lead down on the attackers and drove them off. After this Thomas built a tower on to the house, embattled its walls and in Carew's words 'in a manner made it into a castle'.

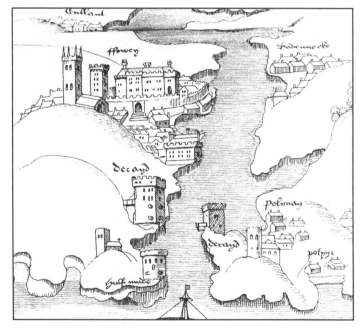

Detail, from the Henry VIII defence map of the south coast of Cornwall, showing Fowey harbour with the well-defended Place, home of the Treffrys, standing out beyond the church.

The Yorkist king, Edward IV, who followed Henry VI, had trouble with a Cornish rebellion against him, and more trouble with Fowey when its 'Gallants' paid no attention to his attempts to impose law and order in the Channel. So in 1474 he impounded its ships and removed the chain which guarded its harbour against attack. It was the start of Fowey's decline as a trading port, and did not endear the Yorkist cause to its merchants, least of all the Treffrys. Small wonder that Thomas Treffry's sons, John and William, joined the other westcountry gentlemen in plotting against King Edward's brother, the crouchback Richard III.

They were among the conspirators who proclaimed Henry Tudor, Earl of Richmond, as king in 1483 but bad weather ruined the uprising. Richmond 'hovered upon the coast' for a spell and went back to Brittany. John and William Treffry fled with other Cornish landowners to join him there.

A modern view of Fowey, with Place still prominent behind the church. The china clay docks can be seen higher up the river.

The two brothers were at Richmond's side when he landed at Milford Haven in 1485 and John was dubbed knight for his services. Richmond marched on to Bosworth Field to defeat Richard and take the throne as Henry VII. The younger Treffry brother William was made Surveyor of Customs for the port of London and then Controller of Coinage for Devon and Cornwall. The first office gave him a finger in the pie of England's greatest port, the second a helping to the riches of the westcountry tin industry. He was also given several manors, and became a gentleman usher at court.

Sir John died in 1500 to be succeeded by this brother William. Both were several times Sheriff of Cornwall and were obviously very capable men, well known and respected at the court of Henry VII. William was kind and generous too. He took great care over the welfare of his heir Thomas, son of his younger brother Thomas. The three brothers are commemorated in Fowey Church with an effigy of brother John in full armour, with brothers William and Thomas on either side in civilian clothes.

Young Thomas Treffry became a friend and regular correspondent of Thomas Cromwell, Henry VIII's right-hand man. He supported the new Protestant religion and, though his family in the past had been benefactors both of Fowey parish church and the nearby Priory of Tywardreath, informed Cromwell of the irreligious conditions at the priory. But he was not rewarded with any spoils from the priory, although he was apppointed surveyor of the castle-building going on at Pendennis, St Mawes and Fowey. Eventually he gave up his post as Collector of Customs for Cornwall (which was becoming a family perquisite) in exchange for the command of St Mawes Castle. Treffy even moved some of the guns from Place to St Mawes. Leland, Henry's antiquarian sent out to report on the condition of the country, stayed at Place with Thomas Treffy.

When King Henry's son Edward VI died in 1553, Thomas was with the other Protestant gentlemen of Cornwall who, fearing the Catholic Mary's accession to the throne, proclaimed Lady Jane Grey as queen. Mary Tudor still took the throne, and had Lady Jane executed. Thomas Treffry had to flee the country. At this time the family seem to have lost much of their estate but Thomas was soon back, and MP for Cornwall in 1555. He lived to see Queen Elizabeth come to the throne, and died in 1563.

His son John remained a power in Cornwall. Spanish treasure ships were seized in Fowey harbour in 1571 as a reply to the Spanish treachery against John Hawkins at San Juan de Ulloa. Half a million pounds worth of gold and plate, destined for Parma's army in the Low Countries, was taken to Place before being moved first to Trematon Castle and then to London. John Treffry was at the execution in Launceston of Cuthbert Mayne, the Catholic priest captured hiding in a Cornish house. It was Treffry who cut short the priest's final speech from the scaffold, ordering the hangman to put the noose about his neck.

John was followed on his death in 1590 by his son William (1559-1603). He was elected MP for Fowey in 1584 and 1596, but in spite of that led the Fowey merchants in protesting at the royal command to contribute to the new fort which Francis Drake was building on Plymouth Hoe. He was in constant correspondence with Robert Cecil, who recommended him as a JP so that he might be able to question suspicious characters arriving at Fowey. He seems to have been the Cornish controller of Cecil's intelligence service. When the country was fearful of further Spanish Armadas, William Treffry became Master of Ordnance under Walter Raleigh's command.

Richard Carew, who had been a close friend of his father, wrote in his *Survey of Cornwall* of 'Mr William Treffry, a gentleman that has vowed his rare gifts of learning, wisdom and courage to the good of his country'.

William died in the same year as Queen Elizabeth and was followed by his nine-year old son John (1594-1658). John married a daughter of the Royalist Sir Arthur Champernowne of Modbury in Devon, which may explain why John joined the king's forces when most other members of his family were Parliamentarian. One cousin was Hugh Peters, the radical Puritan preacher, one of the founders in America of Harvard University. Peters returned to London, became very influential on the Parliamentary side and was executed on the Restoration in 1660. John became a colonel in the Royalist forces. No doubt it was the influence of John Treffry's Parliamentary relations, notably his brother-in-law Jack Trefusis, which saved Place and John from heavy penalties under the Commonwealth.

John was followed at Place by a cousin whose son in turn left the estate in 1731 to his sister's son, William Toller (1676-1735). Toller like his father was a leading Fowey merchant, had served his turn as Mayor and was Collector of Customs in the port. He took the name of Treffry in 1734, the year before his death. His son Thomas (1724-76) also married the daughter of a local merchant and alderman. These eighteenth-century Treffrys who served as members of Parliament and took their turn as High Sheriff seem much more concerned with local trade and politics than with Place, which was sadly neglected. The tower particularly fell into ruin.

William Esco Treffry followed his father but died three years later, in 1779. His heir was the son of his sister who had married John Austen, member of a St Germans family who had become a Plymouth merchant. Susanna Austen took over Place in 1786 with a four-year-old son, Joseph Thomas Austin (1782-1850). She was, says an historian, 'a lady of decided personality', a high Tory who dominated her circle of friends. Among them was John Wolcot (who achieved national fame as the savage satirist Peter Pindar). She remained active and in good health until she died in 1842. Her son emerges as one of the key figures in Cornwall in the first half of the nineteenth century. He was speaking at Reform Movement meetings in 1811 and championed the Fowey opponents of the usual corrupt oligarchy running the small town. By 1813 he had started

rebuilding Place, a task which took most of his life. In 1836, the year he was High Sheriff, he changed his name to Treffry. He was also doing a great deal to restore the family fortunes, which financed his rebuilding.

J. T. Treffry was said to be the major employer of men in the whole westcountry. He owned vast copper mines in mid Cornwall, ships, smelting works and shares in tin and other copper mines when they were at their most productive. He built the harbours at Newquay and Par, and linked the two with a light railway. Then he became the first chairman of the Cornwall Railway, reaching from Penzance to the main line system at Plymouth and linking up the little mineral lines. As such he worked closely with the line's engineer, I.K. Brunel, and was prominently concerned in the decision to cross the Tamar by bridge at Saltash, rather than by ferry link at Torpoint.

J. T. Treffry, 'The King of Mid Cornwall'.

His most visible memorial today is the magnificent Treffry Viaduct across the Luxulyan valley; 660 feet long with ten spans each of 40 feet each; the first granite viaduct built in Cornwall. The most enduring of his enterprises is Par Harbour, built 1829-40 and today the busiest harbour in the whole south-west.

For his rebuilding of Place, J.T. Treffry used Regency Gothic in order to compliment the original Gothic work. He added the two towers and if today the exterior rather looks like a Victorian fantasy, it does incorporate much of the medieval building. Of all the Cornish landowners who went into business in the ninetenth century, J. T. Treffry

The busy china clay port of Par, which was first created by J.T. Treffry in 1829-40.

The Luxulyan Viaduct, always regarded as J.T. Treffry's memorial. It carried a railway line (a train is visible in this drawing) and, under the rails, a pipe carrying the water of a leat across the valley.

was the most brilliant. So wide were his interests that it is no wonder that his affairs were in Chancery for many years after his death in 1850. Nor is it surprising that he had no time to get married.

The estate went to his cousin, the Rev. E.J.Willcocks (1809-1880), headmaster of Berkhamsted School, who at once changed his name to Treffry. He was Vicar of Fowey 1863-7 and of Lansallos 1871-2. Place passed to his son C.E.Treffry (1842-1924) who was a magistrate, took his turn as High Sheriff, and was the first Mayor of Fowey under a new charter in 1913.

His son Edward (1869-1942) followed his father in the Territorial Army. Colonel Treffry, the rank he held on his succession, served in both the South African campaign and First World War. He was the first commanding officer to take the Honorable Artillery Company (Infantry) to serve overseas, and subsequently commanded the 4/5th DCLI (1924-25) and the Devon and Cornwall Infantry Brigade TA 1925-28. His medal ribbons included CMG, OBE, and the Territorial Decoration. The Colonel was vice-lieutenant and chairman of quarter sessions; all in all a formidable figure in the county.

His son, John Esco, born in 1914, also served with the 4/5th DCLI in the Second World War. His great enthusiasm was hunting, and he was master of the Fowey Harriers in 1938, the Axe Vale Harriers 1947-9 and the Burton pack 1958-61.

When the Colonel died in 1942 his widow Anne continued to live at Place until her death in 1985 aged 94. Her father-in-law had inherited the estate in 1880 so two generations spanned a century at Place. Anne Treffry played a leading part in the public life of Fowey and was the only woman to be made an honorary freeman of the borough. In her time the estate was made over to a trust, and on her death the estate was rented by her nephew David Treffry. He had served in the DCLI in the 1939-45 war, the Colonial Service and subsequently the World Bank in New York. He was awarded the OBE, became High Sheriff in 1991 and President of the Royal Institution of Cornwall.

The Treffrys are one of those rare English families which have held their land and their place in local society since medieval times and, apart from a couple of knighthoods, have never been honoured with any title. A very private family, Place is one of the few great houses in the county not open to the public.

Shall Trelawny Die?

The position of Bishop Trelawny as the great Cornish hero owes more to the vigour and appeal of Robert Hawker's nineteenth-century song than to any real Cornish qualities or noble deeds, just as Guy Fawkes owes his fame to fireworks. He was in fact a jovial, hard-drinking seventeenth-century landowner who generally approved of James II until he swung too much to Rome, then opposed him and was consigned to the Tower for his 'sauciness'.

The family takes its name from the manor of Trelawny in Altarnun and claims its descent from the Saxon family who owned it at the time of the Conquest and still held it in 1086, a rare occurrence. Various members were knighted and sat in Parliament over the years but the first to win real fame was John, twice MP for the county, who fought at Agincourt along with that company of Cornishmen whose banner bore the device of two wrestlers. His ransoms from the battle swelled the family fortunes, and its land holdings.

The heads of the family played their part in county life, serving as MPs, sheriffs and coroners, with some being knighted. There was a Trelawny knight templar in the reign of Henry VII. His son John married an heiress and their daughter married Thomas Flamank, the Bodmin lawyer who led the rebellion of the Cornishmen against Henry VII's tax demands in 1497. They were not defeated until they reached Blackheath, and Flamank was duly hanged, drawn and quartered.

John, who died in 1568, served his turn in the various county offices but is remembered for being fined £6 for refusing the honour of knighthood. By this time the family were living at Menheniot but John's son Jonathan (1568-1605) prospered under Queen Elizabeth and bought the estate of Trelawne in Pelynt. There are various stories of trickery in the deal, and it is suggested that that it was bought to give their name a good ring; Trelawny of Trelawne. At any rate, Sir Jonathan also acquired the borough of West Looe, and for bringing its two votes in Parliament to Cecil he was knighted in 1597. His cousin Edward became a Plymouth merchant and that branch of the family became important citizens, settling at Ham

Trelawne, a nineteenth-century engraving.

(where the mansion, sold by Plymouth Corporation to the Anchor Housing Association about 1975, is now carved into flats). The family has provided several mayors of Plymouth.

The next Trelawny of Trelawne, John (1592-1664) was a leader of the 'King's Friends' in Cornwall in the 1620s, opposing the nomination of Sir John Eliot as a knight of the shire and being rewarded with a baronetcy in 1628. He and his son Jonathan (1624-80), the second baronet, were enthusiastic Royalists in the Civil War and afterwards in 1648 were both arrested for plotting in the king's favour. John was sent a prisoner to Plymouth, but Jonathan escaped. Although the family was heavily fined by Parliament for its part in the Civil War, it managed to keep Trelawne.

During the Commonwealth Jonathan was a leading Cornish member of the Sealed Knot, worked closely with John Grenville and acted as a courier to the King in exile. Time and again his treason to the Commonwealth was known, but he always managed to escape arrest.

His eldest son Jonathan (1650-1721), the most famous Trelawny, stayed in holy orders when he became the third baronet. He remained an active supporter of the Stuarts, and set the militia in readiness when Monmouth landed at Lyme Regis in rebellion against his father, King James. Trelawny was ready to march upcountry at their head when news came of Monmouth's capture after the battle of Sedgemoor.

The King at once made him Bishop of Bristol, though Trelawny asked for Exeter, the richer see and the one in which his estates lay. He tolerated the King's growing affection for the Papists until the Declaration of Indulgence, which gave religious freedom to both Roman Catholics and nonconformists. As he was to declare at a later date, he cherished an implacable hatred of 'papists and the furious kind of dissenters'. So he not only refused to sign the second Declaration, but drew up a petition against it.

James sent him, along with six other bishops, to the Tower, declaring that the Bishop of Bristol 'had been most saucy' of them all. He was released on bail within a week, and brought to trial for seditious libel. National uproar followed, and it is said that the cry of 'Shall Trelawny die' arose at this time. When the seven were acquitted there was nationwide rejoicing. Bonfires blazed in Bristol, cannons were fired at Looe and church bells rung at Pelynt.

Trelawny became a passive supporter of William of Orange. James offered to translate him to Exeter in a last effort to keep his loyalty, but it was too late. Trelawny wrote to William saying that he was glad to play his part in the preservation of law, liberty and the Protestant religion. Once on the throne William made him Bishop of Exeter. But again Trelawny changed his tune: he did not approve of William's toleration and fell out with him. For ten years he stayed away from the court. Much of the time he was at Trelawne running his diocese, which covered both Devon and Cornwall, and even made clergy come to him to be ordained. But he went on defending clerical rights against all other power.

By 1701 Bishop Trelawny was back at court, and in 1707 translated to Winchester, to the fury of some people. The broad church Bishop Burnett, who wrote *A History of Our Times* did not approve of Trelawny; he said he drank too much for a bishop, had a stiff temper, was too stern a parent, and cursed like a trooper. Bishop Trelawny's reply was simple: 'When I swear I do not swear as a priest, but as a baronet and a country gentleman'. The convivial, cantankerous old man lived on until 1721, enjoying the best of both roles. If nature imitates art, he is a survivor from a Restoration comedy.

His brother Charles was a similar character. A soldier, he fought for James II against Monmouth, became colonel of the notorious Kirke's Lambs, went over to William of Orange with Kirke and Churchill in 1688, and fought against James II at the Battle of the Boyne. William made him a major-general in 1691 but he resigned in 1692 in protest at William's preference for foreign officers. The Bishop's sons equally made their mark in the world. Two were parsons, one was lost at sea with Sir Clowdisley Shovell, and one was a colonel in the army. Edward, after being a commissioner of customs and MP for the family

Laetitia, daughter of the Bishop: when she grew up she had to overcome her father's fierce opposition before she could marry her cousin Harry.

seat, West Looe, from 1722 to 1735, became Governor of Jamaica in 1738 and made quite a success of it for sixteen years. The eldest son John, the fourth baronet, was MP for both Liskeard and West Looe at varying times, but died without children in 1756.

The title passed to his cousin Harry (1687-1762), the soldier's son, who had married the Bishop's daughter after a long courtship in which Sir Jonathan had strongly opposed the suit. Years of charming love letters survive as a reminder of the romance. Their only son died as a boy at Westminster; their only daughter married her cousin William, the Bishop's grandson. So William became the sixth baronet, a captain in the Royal Navy and then Governor of Jamaica like his uncle. He died in Jamaica in 1772.

One of his grandsons was Edward John Trelawny (1792-1881), the 'Corsair', a romantic from the start, 'beautiful and terrible as a tempest'. Badly treated by his father, he was sent into the navy, deserted in the East Indies and fled to Java in 1811. Back in England after four years, he got married, became a friend of both Byron and Shelley, and just missed accompanying Shelley on his fatal yacht voyage from Leghorn. It was Trelawny who burnt the poet's body on the beach. In 1823 he was off to Greece with Byron to help the fight for independence, left him to join up with a more vigorous rebel chieftain, and went on fighting long after Byron's death. Finally back in England in 1832, this big, handsome hero was lionised as the last link with the great poets.

The mainstream did not quite keep up this pace. The seventh baronet, the Rev. Sir Harry (1756-1834), the Governor of Jamaica's only son, managed to be in turn a Presbyterian minister, an Anglican vicar and a Roman Catholic priest. He tried to teach his tenants the benefits of modern farming methods, like ploughing with horses rather than oxen, but they never listened. Geoffrey Grigson, who grew up in Pelynt, says he was remembered in village folklore as Mad Sir Harry.

His son, the eighth baronet, Sir William (1781-1856), became Lord Lieutenant of Cornwall but in 1802 under the will of a cousin, assumed the surname of Salusbury-Trelawny. His son the ninth baronet, Sir John (1816-85) was twice MP for Tavistock and then for South-East Cornwall. He was followed by his son, Sir William (1844-1917), the tenth baronet, who played the dutiful rounds, deputy-lieutenant, magistrate, sheriff twice. He was also the last baronet to live at Trelawne.

Between 1913 and 1925 the Salusbury-Trelawnys sold up their Cornish estates, and last of all the house. It became the Home of St Barnabas for retired clergy of the Church of England (a Roman Catholic daughter gave sanctuary to a Catholic order of Poor Clares just a few hundred yards from Trelawne).

A few years ago the clergy retired from Trelawne, and the house became a country club and entertainment centre, surrounded now by caravans, swimming pool, children's slides and swings.

So the family had moved away from Cornwall by the end of the First World War. They still prosper; the current head of the family, the thirteenth baronet, prefers to be known simply as Sir John Trelawny. He spent his formative years at Looe (West Looe was once almost part of the estate), went to sea as a Merchant Navy apprentice before the war, was commissioned in the Royal Navy and served mainly in Coastal Forces. Professionally he is chairman of the country's leading executive search consultancy, still spends time in Cornwall most years and

The swimming pool at Trelawne; a 'holiday village' is now established at the home of the Cornish hero, Bishop Trelawny.

is a member of the London Cornish Society. He gets to Pelynt for the annual Trelawny Day, and has strong links with the Cornwall County Rugby Supporters Association - known as 'Trelawny's Army'.

The Romantic Trevanions

Like so many Cornish families, the Trevanions were content for generation after generation to go along quietly; yet when they did break out they could become the most splendid and glamorous heroes of romance. As the name suggests, they are native Cornish, originating at Trevanion, in the same parish as Caerhays, which came into the family in the reign of Edward III through a marriage with an Arundell heiress.

They rose enough in the late fifteenth century to be linked with the Lancastrian Edgcumbe in bringing down the powerful Bodrugan after Henry VII reached the throne. In reward for their loyalty they were given manors on the Fal and near St Austell.

'The athletic Sir William', a master of jousting, was a great favourite of Henry VIII, three times Sheriff of Cornwall and, financially rewarding, controller of tin for Devon and Cornwall. In the campaign against the French which led to the Battle of the Spurs, Sir William commanded a succession of ships, including in 1513 the biggest royal ship, the *Gabriel Royal* which carried 600 men.

William died in 1512. His son, Sir Hugh, was equally loyal to Henry and a good Protestant. He was one of the leaders of the small Cornish forces sent against the Yorkshire uprising known as the Pilgrimage of Grace in 1542, and a member first of the commission appointed to clear up Cornwall after the 1549 Prayer Book Rebellion, and then to collect all unnecessary church silver in 1552. The Trevanions continued as leaders of the county right through Elizabethan times.

As the struggle between King Charles and Parliament developed, it was John (1614-43), the Trevanion eldest son, who commanded attention. He was MP for Lostwithiel in the Long Parliament, supporting the King and voting against the attainder of Strafford in 1641. When the Civil War broke out John was one of the King's commissioners for the militia, and as soon as a Cornish army was formed he raised a regiment which the family maintained at its own expense. When that army began its victorious campaign in 1642, Trevanion was at the head of his men all the way, fighting through every battle until he was mortally wounded in the capture of Bristol.

It was a Pyrrhic victory, for all the great leaders of the Cornishmen fell in the action. Trevanion was only twenty-nine, 'a man of good understanding, great courage but of few words, yet of what he said has always been to the purpose'.

Charles, his father, was active as vice-admiral of the south coast of Cornwall. He was knighted by King Charles at Boconnoc before the Lostwithiel triumph, and took to the field in spite of his age in the last stages of the war, opposing the advance of Fairfax. A few years later he was arrested with other Cornish leaders, suspected of plotting against Parliament. His estate was sequestered, and only the heavy fine of £658 redeemed it.

Sir Charles did not live to see the Restoration but his heir was Charles, one of John's four sons. He was MP for Grampound from 1661 to 1679. Both his two brothers were naval captains; one died in the third Dutch War. The other,

Caerhays: a winter view seen over the lake.

Richard, carried James II into exile. He was with James at his vain attempt to win back Ireland which ended at the Battle of the Boyne, and again escorted him into final exile. He became groom of the bedchamber at St Germain, and was with James II when he died in 1701.

After 1688 John (1670-1740), who succeeded his father in 1703, spent much money in improving (though not rebuilding) Caerhays and its gardens, rather as those other

Tories, the Carews, were doing at Antony. John sat for Tregony and then for Bodmin as a Tory for a few years. He married a daughter of Lord Berkeley, and her sister married the fourth Lord Byron, thus beginning a fateful union.

The eldest son of this Lord Byron was 'the wicked Lord Byron', who killed his man in a duel, was ostracised by society and shut himself up in Newstead Abbey. The wicked lord's brother John went into the navy and after remarkable adventures as a youngster rose rapidly to

Sophia Trevanion, who married Captain (later Admiral) John Byron, and was the poet's grandmother.

captain. In 1748 he married his cousin Sophia Trevanion, sister of the young William who had succeeded their father in 1740. The wedding was in the chapel at Caerhays. Byron had an extensive if undistinguished naval career, ending as an admiral. In his long absences at sea Sophie, rather a blue stocking, made a considerable name for herself in London society, being prominent in the circle of Mrs Montagu, Mrs Boscawen (the wife of that other Cornish admiral), Mrs Thrale and Dr Johnson.

Their second son, George, was a successful frigate captain who died young. The eldest son, Jack Byron, was a disaster, eloping with a marchioness, then marrying a Scots heiress for her money. Their offspring was George Gordon, the sixth Lord Byron, the most notorious poet in our history. Thus his grandmother was Sophia Trevanion, and he was always friendly with his Trevanion cousins.

A.L.Rowse has thoroughly examined Byron's Cornish background in his book *The Trevanions and Byrons*. Rowse believes that the poet's father was the lover of his sister Fanny. The poet himself was the lover of his half-sister Augusta. Augusta married her sixteen-year-old daughter Georgina off to young Henry Trevanion, second son of the last Trevanion to live at Caerhays. He gave his wife four children and then ran off with his fifteen-year-old sister-in-law Medora and gave her two children in a tempestuous affair. The Trevanions and the Byrons between them produced a heady mixture.

John Trevanion, whose daughter Sophia was the wife of Admiral Byron, left another daughter and a son William. This William (1728-1767), for most of his adult life MP for Tregony, died without children and left Caerhays to his sister Sophie Byron and her elder sister, Frances. She had married an ecclesiastical lawyer, John Bettesworth. Frances died before her brother so on his death Caerhays passed to her son, another John Bettesworth. John died in 1789, leaving as heir a nine-year-old boy, John Trevanion Purnel Bettesworth (1780-1840). He took the surname of Trevanion when he came of age in 1801, was sheriff a few

The poet Byron, who kept close contact with his Trevanion cousins.

London for Prinny. He laid out the route up Regent Street to Regent's Park, turned Buckingham House into a palace and built the Marble Arch as its entrance. All this was in the future when John Trevanion brought him to Caerhays in 1808. He wanted an extravagant, romantic castle with elegant gardens leading down to the water's edge at the foot of the hill.

It was all too grandiose. As this Regency fantasy grew so the estate dwindled. Bit by bit it was sold off to pay the ever-mounting bills. By 1824 practically all the estate had been sold off, or mortgaged. John Trevanion was hopelessly in debt and so he disappeared to Brussels, presumably to escape his creditors. There he died in 1840, and in 1853 the unfinished castle, mortgaged and remortgaged, was sold to John Michael Williams of Scorrier, of the most successful tin mining families in the county.

A final irony is that land sold off at St Stephen-in-Brannel, and the Treverbyn estate also near St Austell, turned out to be on nearly solid china clay. Certainly the Rockingham Gill family, of the London solicitors Gill & Irving, who bought Treverbyn, lived on their royalties for over a century.

But the family went from Cornwall, and more or less quietly drifted out of sight. There is a story that the last of the Trevanions at Caerhays would amuse himself after dinner in the unfinished splendour of his house by shooting out with a pistol the eyes of the family portraits around the walls. The early Trevanions were capable of producing dashing, lovable creatures. The introduction of Byron blood seems to have been fatal.

years later and for a short spell MP for Penryn, but the young man had big ideas.

He brought in the fashionable architect John Nash, the Prince Regent's favourite. Nash redesigned half west

95

Vivians of Glynn

Most visitors to Cornwall drive through the Glynn Valley, that wonderful wooded stretch beside the Fowey river between Doublebois and Bodmin. Few see the old house of Glynn gleaming away to the north, as they approach Bodmin Parkway station. The Vivians were established there by a Waterloo hero; but by the end of the Second World War they had to sell up.

Vivians claim old Cornish blood; there is a suggestion that the last Prior of Bodmin was of their family. They had been in St Columb in the reign of Henry VII. In the seventeenth century Thomas Vivian married Mary Glynn. John Vivian of Truro, called the 'father of the copper trade' in the eighteenth century, became Vice-Warden of the Stannaries. With Francis Basset he set up the Cornish Metal Company, which from 1785 until 1792 tried to buy all the copper being produced in Cornwall. Then he moved to Swansea and set up a copper smelting works. He had two sons, John Henry who stayed in Swansea running the business, and Richard Hussey Vivian, who used his father's wealth to establish an army career.

The two brothers were joint owners of the smelting works, but it was John Henry's son, Henry Hussey Vivian(1821-94), who built up the Hafod Works, and indeed Swansea, into 'the metallurgical centre of the world'. There were a series of actions against the copper smelters for the pollution they caused – four farms downwind of Hafod had to be abandoned – but the Welsh juries never found against the companies. He played a leading part in improving Swansea's harbour facilities and creating a rail link with the Rhondda. After the coal strike of 1889 he originated the scale of sliding wages which settled all disputes with miners for many years.

Henry Vivian was MP for Truro 1852-57, and then represented Welsh seats until made Lord Swansea in 1893. He was the first Chairman of Glamorgan County Council from 1889 until his death five years later. The barony still flourishes.

The first Lord Swansea's uncle, Lieutenant-General Sir Richard Hussey Vivian, GCB, first Baron Vivian (1775-1842), had two terms at Oxford, two years in France learning the language, a couple months in Devonport articled to a solicitor, Jonathan Elford, and then went into the army. He saw service in the Low Countries, gained rapid promotion (in the days when rank was obtained by purchase) and by 1802 was a major, by 1804 a lieutenant-colonel. That year he married the daughter of Philip Champion de Crespigny, of a distinguished French Huguenot family who had fled to England after 1685.

By now Vivian had transferred from a line regiment into the cavalry, and went to Portugal in 1808 in command of the 7th Light Dragoons. In Moore's epic retreat to Corunña he distinguished himself in the rearguard. 1813 saw him back in the Peninsula, landing at Bilbao in command of a brigade and advancing in support of Wellington at Vittoria. He saw much fighting under the Duke and returned wounded to England with the great man's commendations.

Back in Brussels in 1815 as a major general, he was at the Duchess of Richmond's ball; marched out that night to Quatre Bras and the next day after much fighting led his

Glynn House in the nineteenth century.

brigade in the final charge at Waterloo.

In 1825 he bought Glynn, no doubt prompted by thoughts of his maternal ancestor. The family of Glynn had lost the estate in the fourteenth century but in 1805 it was bought back by Edmund John Glynn, son of a Recorder of London. He is described as a young man of great ability and learning who for years never spoke, communicating with others by writing. He built a large Georgian house on the site of the old mansion. After it was completed an uncle had Edmund declared a lunatic, and so gained the new house for himself. Soon after, in 1791, fire reduced the new house to a burnt-out shell. These ruins General Vivian bought. He rebuilt it, with additions.

He was an MP from 1825 to 1831, for Truro and then Windsor. But his heart was still in the cavalry: when he was made baronet in 1828 the supporters he took in his arms were a lancer and a hussar, both mounted and in full figure. Then in 1831 he became Commander-in-Chief Ireland. In May 1935, after refusing to become Secretary for War, he was made Master-General of the Ordnance. He then became a peer in 1841. The next year he died suddenly in Baden-Baden.

His eldest son, Sir Robert Hussey Vivian (1802-87), was born out of wedlock but brought up as a member of the family. He joined the East India Company's army, saw a great deal of active service and by 1854, when he finally returned to England, was a major-general. The next year he commanded the Turkish contingent in the Crimea, was knighted on his return and appointed to the newly-formed Council of India.

His younger brother, the second baron, Charles de Crespigny Vivian (1808-86), retired from the army as a major in 1834, was MP for South-East Cornwall from 1835 until he succeeded to the barony in 1842, and was Lord Lieutenant of the county from 1856 until 1877. The third brother, John, was an MP for Truro and held minor government offices.

The third baron, Hussey Crespigny Vivian (1834-93) spent a life in the Diplomatic Service, serving eventually as ambassador to Copenhagen, Brussels and finally Rome where he died in office. He is described as 'conscientious but not brilliant'. It was his two sisters who shone, Violet and Doris, 'the beautiful Vivian twins'. Violet was a maid-of-honour to Queen Victoria and later lady-in-waiting to Queen Alexandra from 1901 to 1925. Doris also served in the household of both these monarchs and of Queen Elizabeth the Queen Mother. Doris married Field Marshall Earl Haig, Commander of the British Army in the First World War.

George Crespigny Vivian DSO, the fourth baron (1878-1940), was a major in the 17th Lancers, seeing active service in both the South African War (when he was severely wounded) and in the First World War. He was an ADC to the King of the Belgians, and later to King George VI.

Daphne Glynn in the 1920s; she very much embodied the spirit of the time.

Later he commanded both the 4th/5th Duke of Cornwall's Light Infantry and the Royal 1st Devon Yeomanry, and was chairman of the Cornwall Territorial Army Association.

In all these years Glynn saw little of them. The diplomat third baron never lived there, and for thirty years the house was let to Edward St Aubyn. Not until the outbreak of the Second World War did the fourth baron decide to live there. He died in 1940.

His children, Daphne and Anthony, accustomed from an early age to tea parties and the like in royal surroundings through their aunts, were among the brightest of bright young things in the 1920s. Daphne, born in 1904, married the heir to the fifth Marquess of Bath secretly in 1926, and officially the next year. After producing the sixth marquess's remarkable sons (including the present Marquess of Bath) the marriage broke up and Daphne married Xan Fielding, the hero of Cretan resistance in the Second World War. They led a bohemian life, described in two vivid autobiographies by Daphne. In the first, *Mercury Presides*, she claims the rare distinction of having been

Dr Peter Mitchell, the Nobel prizewinner, in front of Glynn House in 1990.
He has established it as the base of the Glynn Research Foundation.

potted by Queen Alexandra at a Palace party.

The 5th Lord Vivian, who has died aged 85, became a national celebrity in 1954, when he was shot in the abdomen by Mavis Wheeler, the former wife of Sir Mortimer Wheeler and the former mistress of Augustus John.

So begins the *Daily Telegraph* obituary of Anthony (1906-91), the fifth baron. The couple seem to have been living together, but the events of the day were never really sorted out. The lady went to prison but Anthony waited for her. He had a mixed career; theatre manager, leader of a couple of London dance bands, special constable during the Second World War, partner with C.B. Cochran in producing 'Bless the Bride', among other shows. But he eventually lost all his money in the theatre, managed various restaurants and had odd brushes with the police.

By 1947 Anthony could no longer afford Glynn and the estate was sold. For twenty years it lay empty. Daphne described her last visit there in 1955, the main drive a jungle of rhododendrons, chickens in the hall, holes in the roof letting in water. The house was bought by Dr Peter Mitchell, a biochemist, in 1962. He restored and rebuilt it, and in 1974 made it the base of the Glynn Research Foundation. His work on energy in biology, the chemiosmotic theory, earned him the Nobel Prize for Chemistry in 1978.

The barony goes on. Anthony's son Nicholas Crespigny, now the sixth Lord Vivian, born in 1935, joined the Army like so many of his ancestors. He commanded the 16th/5th Lancers 1976-79, held various staff appointments subsequently and became a brigadier in 1987. His heir is Charles Hussey Crespigny Vivian, born in 1966.

At Glynn the plaster replicas of the decorations, both English and foreign, of the dashing cavalry commander who established the family there, still glow from the ceiling of the state rooms. They look down, however, on a different world.

Vyvyans of Trelowarren

The Vyvyans, one of the oldest families in Cornwall, hailed originally from St Buryan in the wild country west of Penzance, and a wild family they were: assault, murder and wrecking are all on their charge sheets. One was even excommunicated. But they settled down and became respectable after 1426 when John married the heiress of Trelowarren, in the softer country at the head of the Helford river.

His son Richard was Sheriff of Cornwall a couple times in Henry VII's reign, and his grandson Michael was Sheriff and the first captain of St Mawes Castle, then nearing

The Tudor castle at St Mawes, where the Vyvyans almost held the governorship as an inheritance, after Michael was the first captain.

completion. Richard had married an Arundell of Trerice; Michael's son John married a co-heir of the Earl of Devon. The family was not only respectable but adding vast estates to its fortune. John began to rebuild the medieval mansion at Trelowarren.

The next John was an MP for Helston; his son Hannibal was an important man in the county in the vital Elizabethan years of war with Spain. He was governor of St Mawes Castle, vice-admiral of the Southern Shore, and constantly in correspondence with Walter Raleigh about the defence of the county. He was an MP for Helston, Truro and St Mawes in the reign of Elizabeth and on into James's reign.

Richard, his son, was knighted at a court masque in 1636, the year in which he married Mary Bulteel of Barnstaple. He too busied himself with enlarging Trelowarren, but this was halted by the Civil War. Sir Richard was an immediate leader of the Cornish Royalists, as a colonel of the militia. In 1642 he was given command of a new fort on St Dennis Head, at the entrance to the Helford river, and bore the cost of building the fort.

The next year he was authorised with Jonathan Rashleigh to collect plate donated by Cornish gentry for the Royalist cause, and set up a mint at Truro to make currency from it. Very soon he took charge of the mint at Exeter, ending the Truro operation. He made one foray west from Exeter in 1644, accompanying the king on his triumphant advance into Cornwall. When a number of Cornish gentlemen were knighted at Boconnoc, Richard alone was made a baronet. Back in Exeter his wife was a lady-in-waiting to Queen Henrietta Maria.

He only surrendered to the Parliamentary forces when Fairfax took Exeter in 1646, and for years after had a miserable life, harried with lawsuits and harrassed with fines for his Royalist activities. All told the war cost him nearly £10 000.

But all was well after the Restoration. Sir Richard was deputy-lieutenant of the county, governor of St Mawes, and able to get on with enlarging Trelowarren. His son, Sir Vyell, the second baronet, briefly MP for Helston and sheriff in his turn, died without children in 1696 and Trelowarren passed to his nephew, another Richard.

Sir Richard Vyvyan, created baronet during King Charles's one visit to the county during the Civil War.

This Sir Richard, the third baronet, was a county MP in Queen Anne's reign, and produced six sons and four daughters. These children founded long and fecund lines: one descendant Jennifer Vyvyan (1925-74) won fame in our own time as a great operatic soprano, creating many leading roles in modern operas and singing with the leading companies.

But Sir Richard was a rabid Jacobite: in 1715 the Hanoverian king sent messengers to arrest him. Warned of their approach Sir Richard was able to destroy many incriminating papers but was still arrested and had a spell in the Tower

For the rest of the century the Vyvyans kept quiet. Sir Vyell (1767-1820), the seventh baronet, planted the original gardens and in keeping with the taste of his day gave the chapel its elegant Gothic interior.

The family Jacobitism had turned into high Toryism. The eighth baronet, Sir Richard (1800-79), who succeeded to the title when he was twenty, won a county seat in an 1820 by-election and promptly showed his colours: opposing Catholic emancipation and any kind of reform in Parliament. He was returned for the county in 1826 and 1830, but in that Parliament declared his intention of weakening Wellington's government as much as possible. He played his part in the Duke's resignation, and then would not support his Whig replacement. The House was in uproar with Sir Richard in the thick of the battle.

Parliament was dissolved: for five days Vyvyan fought for his county seat and then threw in the sponge. But he got into Parliament for the rotten borough of Okehampton in 1831 and 1832, and was returned by Bristol in 1835 after highly expensive elections. He fought reform of the municipal corporations in 1835 but when defeated again lost interest, and for four years was out of Parliament.

He was back in 1841 as MP for Helston, where his family had held the patronage for centuries, but was still the rebel Tory. Ardent now for protection, he voted against Peel on the repeal of the Corn Laws, and voted against Disraeli's budget in 1852. He retired from Parliament in 1857, content at Trelowarren with his fine library and his woods. He dabbled in geology and physics, was created a Fellow of the Royal Society, wrote many papers on metaphysics and even a paper for the Royal Institute of Cornwall on the large fogou on his property.

The bachelor Sir Richard died in 1879, leaving an estate much mortgaged and encumbered. He was followed by his nephew, the Rev. Sir Vyell (1826-1917), the ninth baronet and Rector of Withiel. The parson's son and the tenth baronet was a soldier, Sir Courtenay (1858-1941). He served in the South African War of 1879, the Matabele War of 1896, the South African War (where he was second-in-command to Baden-Powell in the defence of Mafeking) and the First World War. Sir Courtenay was regularly mentioned in dispatches and finally made CMG. He was brevet colonel of the Buffs (Royal East Kents).

His wife Clara, whom he married in 1929, is better remembered as C.C.Vyvyan for her many books on Cornwall. In *The Old Place* she tells of her struggle to rescue the gardens of Trelowarren after the years of neglect and vandalism in the Second World War, when the house was requisitioned. During this time she created a market garden to help pay expenses. Lady Vyvyan died in 1976.

Trelowarren, the home since 1426 of the Vyvyans.

Sir Courtenay was followed as twelfth baronet by his nephew Sir Richard (1891-1978) who in turn was succeeded by a cousin Sir John, born in 1916. John's grandfather is still remembered as Chief Constable of Devon 1907-31, and his father, Major-General Ralph Vyvyan, was a distinguished signals officer.

Sir John was with the British-American Tobacco Company before the Second World War. During the war he served as a signals officer in Arakan and Bangalore, ending as a major on the staff of the Second Army. He went back to the tobacco company for a few years and then moved to Canada where he worked with the government of British Columbia.

On his succeeding to Trelowarren it became clear that the estate would have to earn money to survive. So an area, well away from the house, was let to the Camping Club, and a wing of the house and the chapel were leased to the Trelowarren Fellowship, an ecumenical trust. Since then a restaurant has been started in the courtyard, and there is a craft gallery and pottery. All the commercial ventures have been successful. In 1983 Sir John made the house over to his son, R.F.A. Vyvyan, who now runs the place, while he retired to Trelowarren Mill.

So, after five hundred years, the family still goes strong in its old house, a fascinating mixture of styles from medieval to Regency Gothic. It is still privately owned and lived in, but the public can go there for a meal and enjoy the crafts on show. And the Vyvyan Arms in Trelowarren Street, Camborne remembers the family influence in the neighbourhood.

The Mining Williams

In the early eighteenth century two Welsh brothers called Williams migrated to Cornwall: they had some mining experience and came to seek their fortune in the new Cornish mining boom. John, the elder, hitched his wagon to a rising star, William Lemon, who by the time Williams appeared was working the Gwennap mines, south-east of Redruth, on an unprecedented scale.

John Williams (c.1684-1761) became manager of Lemon's immensely rich Poldice mine and settled at Burncoose, close by. Mines were getting deeper and draining them was the major problem which Williams promptly took in hand. He began driving what became known as the Great Adit – or drainage channel – from Poldice mine to Bissoe Bridge, over four miles. By the time John Williams had finished, twenty years later, the complete drainage system with all its branches was thirty miles long and drained fifty mines. It made mining possible to depths of eighty fathoms and was ready for the next major development, the steam pumping engines.

John Williams was one of the most successful and extensive managers and adventurers – the men who put their money into mining ventures – in the county. In his long life in mining he introduced many practical improvements. He founded a dynasty which played a dominant part in mining for the next two centuries.

The Williams family was one of the toughest in a bustling, battling age. The area in which they settled, north of Gwennap, came to be called the richest square mile in the Old World. They spread their interests far and

Michael Williams, who built up the Swansea copper smelting business and was High Sheriff of Glamorgan in 1840.

wide. John's grandson, another John, supplemented the old man's Great Adit by building in 1809 the first horse-drawn tramway in the county, from Poldice to Portreath. The landlord, Lord de Dunstanville, was the biggest shareholder. Later another tramway was laid to the south coast ports. They had financial interests in several Cornish banks.

John had sulphur mines in Wicklow, in Ireland, and when in 1806 he bought the manor of Calstock he took an interest in the manganese mining there. In 1810 he became a partner in the Cornish Bank at Truro, and in 1812 when Plymouth Breakwater was starting he and Robert Fox of Falmouth got the contract for quarrying at Oreston the stone for its construction.

Copper needed much coal for its smelting, and it was cheaper to move the ore to South Wales to the coal, than to bring the coal to Cornwall. So in 1831 the Williams family and their associates bought the Morfa Works in Swansea. By mid-century Morfa and the Vivian's Hafod works were two of the big four works which dominated British copper output, and Swansea was responsible for ninety per cent of the world's copper. The Williams Foster company was among the survivors as late as 1914, when the trade was nearly extinct.

Because the coinage laws forced tin to be smelted in the county, so tin smelting was developed in Cornwall. When coinage was abolished in 1839 smelting continued at the established works and, anticipating a big surge in output, the Williams family joined with John's wife's family, the Harveys of Hayle, in 1838 to take over Trethelan tin smelting works near Truro. Later on they took over the Fox works at Perran Wharf and became one of the leading tin smelters in the country, rivalling the Bolithos at Chyandour and keeping that position until the 1920s. From 1850 onwards smelting was the most valuable part of the Williams's mining empire. It also gave them tremendous power in every branch of mining.

The Williams had a finger in many pies: John for instance was the manager of a large number of mines in the Gwennap area before the year 1800. The biggest, Consolidated, was the richest copper mine in the whole world. By 1824 the parish was producing over a third of world's total copper output, and by 1841 it was the most populous area in Cornwall, with more people than Truro or any other town in the county. By this time the family had become joint owners of the Cornish Bank in Truro along with the Tweedy family. Then copper was found overseas, easier and cheaper to mine, and by 1870 the last of the Gwennap copper mines had given up.

Tin came back for a last burst, and George Williams was chairman of Dolcoath, a great Gwennap copper mine in its early days, but now yielding deep tin. In 1888 it paid its highest ever dividend, £58 750, and George gave a champagne dinner to his shareholders. But by 1896, when George's brother M.H.Williams was chairman, even Dolcoath was losing money. Williams withdrew all his capital from Dolcoath, and announced that he was giving up all his holdings in Cornish mines. It signalled the end.

John (1753-1841), grandson of the first John Williams, only inherited £1000 from his father but by the age of twenty-two was manager of Wheal Maiden, and by 1783 was making so much money out of mine management that he built a new house, Scorrier, between Redruth and Chacewater on the northern fringe of Gwennap. He was recognised as the greatest living authority on mining.

His second son Michael (1784-1858) moved into Scorrier House. The family importance in South Wales through the Swansea smelting works was such that he became High Sheriff of Glamorgan in 1840. He was MP for West Cornwall 1853-8, senior Deputy Lieutenant of the county and Deputy Warden of the Stannaries.

But it was his eldest son, John Michael, who made the major change in the family. In 1853 he bought the half-finished Caerhays castle from the bankrupt John Trevanion, completed it and henceforward it became the main Cornish house of the family. His younger brother

*John Michael Williams, who bought Caerhays
in 1853 and completed the building.*

*John Charles Williams, the great gardener
whose williamsii rhododendrons and camellias
feature in every plantsman's catalogue.*

George took over Scorrier House, which he extensively rebuilt: it was described as 'agreeable and commodious'.

John Michael's eldest son Michael (1857-1899) was followed by his brother John Charles (1861-1939), who was Lord Lieutenant of the county from 1981 till 1936. All these Williams, as well as younger brothers, shared the county honours, becoming High Sheriffs, magistrates, Deputy Lieutenants in turn.

But John Charles Williams has a different fame. As the great plant collectors sent their rhododendrons, camellias and magnolias back to England from China and Asia, so he realised that the climate and soil at Caerhays was especially suited to them. He planted their seeds and raised hybrids. Now *williamsii* camellias and hybrids of all these shrubs bearing the name of J.C.Williams or Caerhays are found everywhere in modern gardens. He was generous with his time and knowledge, and many other great gardens in Cornwall still pay tribute to his generosity.

John Charles Williams' son was the Rt Hon. Charles Williams (1886-1952), a lieutenant-commander in the RNVR in the First World War World, MP for Tavistock 1918-22 and then for Torquay for over thirty years, 1924-55. He was appointed a Deputy Speaker in 1945 and made a privy councillor in 1952. He married a daughter of the old family rivals, the Bolithos, but they had no children. His younger brother, Commander A.M.Williams CBE, DSC (1897-1985), had gone into the Royal Navy and saw service in both world wars. He settled at Werrington Park, near Launceston, where the house was built by Sir William Morice, Charles II's secretary of state. Commander Williams was MP for North Cornwall 1924-29 and he too followed his forebears in county honours.

His eldest son Robert took over Werrington Park and his second son, Julian (born 1927) inherited Caerhays in 1955. He was High Sheriff in 1968 and has been Chairman of Cornwall County Council. Julian has two sons Charles and David.

The Baronets

So the family line had divided in modern times, as happened 150 years ago. Then the third son of the second John, William (1791-1870), proved as much of a go-getter as his father. He built himself a house, Tregullow, close to Scorrier House. As the copper boom came to end he made money out of the closing down of the Gwennap mines. He was made a baronet in 1866, oddly enough the year of copper's final collapse in the area.

The second baronet, his eldest son Sir Frederick Martin (1830-1878), shared his father's mining interests and by the end of 1874 was the only family shareholder in the Cornish Bank. Then he died suddenly from a stroke in 1878 at a time when the mining industry was beginning to fail and banks in other parts of the country were collapsing. Without the Williams's support the Cornish Bank was in trouble, and early in 1879 closed its doors. Every bank in Cornwall was under presure in the panic. The West Cornwall Bank at Redruth, owned by John Michael Williams of Caerhays, rode out the storm, and the Williams, Williams and Grylls bank at Falmouth survived after their London agents sent down £2000 in gold sovereigns – popular rumour had it to be a trainload of gold! Later on the Cornish Bank was revived with the Tweedy family in charge, but for a long time there was a rumour (never substantiated) that bad blood between the two branches of the Williams family had largely caused the panic which swept across Cornwall for those hectic weeks.

Sir William's son William Robert (1860-1903), became the third baronet at the age of ten. He played his part in county affairs like his father and grandfather. After that

the title passed swiftly through three brothers until on the death of the eighth baronet William (1907-1960) the title passed to a Canadian kinsman. So this line moved from Cornwall.

At Caerhays Julian continues his father's deep interest in gardening, and like so many of his forebears has performed his share of county duties.

Julian Williams, as High Sheriff of Cornwall in 1968, leads the Lord Lieutenant, the late Sir John Carew Pole, in procession at Truro.

Acknowledgements

In compiling this book I have tried not to bother members of the various families I have been concerned with, but in a few cases this has been necessary. I was always received courteously and kindly, and given much help. In some cases I sent them copies of my essays on their families, and was encouraged by the fact that they found no errors of fact, only in some cases of taste or emphasis. This persuaded me that the other essays might be accurate; where I fail or fall short I apologise.

People who were kind enough to help me in this way were Lord St Levan, Sir Arscott Molesworth-St Aubyn, Sir Richard Rashleigh, Mr and Mrs Prideaux-Brune, Mr Charles Fox and Mr David Treffry. I also turned for help to old friends, Sir Richard Carew Pole, the Hon Robert Eliot, Don Rickard of Fowey, Jack Nash who helped in Penzance and John Booker, the archivist of Lloyds Bank. Librarians as ever have been generous with their time, Mr Knight and Mrs Olds of the Cornwall Studies Library at Redruth, the staff at Torpoint County Library, John Elliot, the West Devon Librarian, and the staff of the Local Studies Library at Pymouth. My thanks to them all.

Finally, the choice of families: there are many 'could-bes'; some are in and some are not. The choice was mine; it would not be everybody's. Where I am wrong, either in leaving out important people, or putting in others and getting things wrong, then I am to blame, by myself.

Photographs and drawings are reproduced by kind permission of the following: I am grateful to so many people, owners of houses, staffs of societies, professional photographers, who all did their utmost to help. The source of each coloured illustration is given in the caption. Lieut-Col E.T. Bolito (Mr J.E.G. Scobie), Brian Errington, 12, 13 top and bottom. Christian Browning, 52, 67. Cornish Studies Library (Joanne Gillman), ii, 2, 8, 37, 54, 57, 69, 97, 103. English China Clays, 86. Gill collection, 42, 46, 47, 82. Haven Leisure, 91. Peter Horder collection, 13 bottom. Lady Molesworth St Aubyn, 59, 60, 61, 77. Mount Edgcumbe Joint Committee (Mrs M. Campbell-Culver), 29, 30. National Maritime Museum, 18. National Trust Regional Office (Liz Luck), 6, 24, 31, 74, 75. A.F. Kersting, 21. Graeme Fowey, 22. Camera Craft, 73. Andrew Besley, 81. John Hicks, Clemens Bodmin, Plymouth Art Gallery, Robert Chapman, 72. Mr Peter Prideaux-Brune, 65. Royal Institution of Cornwall (Roger Penhallurick, Anne Knight and Angela Broome), iv, 3, 4, 43, 44, 68 left. The Earl of St Germans (Mrs Hilary Stevens). Mrs. M. Schofield. Mr W. Fox-Smith, 95. Mr David Treffry, Graeme Fowey, 86. Sir John Trelawny, iii, 90. *Western Morning News* 5, 10 bottom, 14, 17, 20 right, 23, 25, 27 left, 28 top, 37, 40, 48, 68 right, 71, 83, 99, 108. Robert Roskrow, 15. John Rapson, 35. James Tremain, 40. Mr Julian Williams, Jim Matthews, 105, 107 left and right.

Reproduced from books:
Betjamin and Rowse. *Victorian and Edwardian Cornwall*, 79
Britton & Brayley. *Devon and Cornwall Illustrated*, 9 top, 64, 78, 101.
Borlase, *Natural History of Cornwall*, 9 bottom.
Cornish Magazine, 1898-9, 20 left and centre.
Dimont, Elisabeth, *Godolphin Family Portraits* (RIC), 43.
Gay, Susan, *Old Falmouth* (RIC).
Glynn, Daphne, *Mercury Presides*, 98.
Rowse, A.L., *Byrons and Trevanions*, 94.
Saunders, Andrew, *Devon and Cornwall*, 87.
Trewin, Wendy, *Journals of Caroline Fox*, 38.
Vivian, Stanley, *Story of the Vivians*, 102.

References

General

Barton, D.B., *Copper Mining in Devon & Cornwall*. Truro 1968
    History of Tin Mining and Smelting in Cornwall. Truro,
    1965
Boase, G.C., *Collectania Cornubiensia*. 1890
Burke's Extinct Peerages
Burke's Landed Gentry
Burke's Peerage
Carew, Richard, *The Survey of Cornwall* etc., ed. Halliday, F.E.,1953
Coate, Mary, *Cornwall in the Great Civil War*, Oxford 1933
Dictionary of National Biography
Elliott-Binns, L.E., *Medieval Cornwall*, 1955
Halliday, F.E., *History of Cornwall*, 1959
Lake's Parish History of Cornwall
Lawrence, W.T, *Parliamentary Representation of Cornwall*,Truro
Leland, *Itinerary*
McCabe, Helen, *Houses and Gardens of Cornwall*, Padstow, 1988
Pevsner, Nikolaus, *Buildings of England; Cornwall*, 1951
Rowe, John, *Cornwall in the Age of the Industrial Revolution*,
    Liverpool, 1953
Rowse, A.L., *Tudor Cornwall*, 1941
Salmon, Arthur L., *Little Guide to Cornwall*, revised by Ronald
    Hicks, 1950
Tregellas, Walter H., *Worthies of Cornwall*, 1884
Vivian, J.L., *Visitation of Cornwall*, 1887
Who Was Who?
Who's Who?

Introduction

Tangye, Nigel. *The Story of Glendurgal*, Truro, 1962

Bolitho

Cornish Magazine & Devon Miscellany, Vol 1, 1885.
Matthews, W.P.,*History of Barclays Bank*, 1926
Pool, P.A.S., *History of Penzance*, 1974

Boscawen

Aspinal-Oglander, Cecil, *Admiral's Wife*, 1940
    Admiral's Widow, 1942
Norway, Arthur H., 'Admiral. Boscawen, Old Dreadnought.'
    Cornish Magazine, vol 2, p89, 1899
Sachs, E.T., 'The Magpie Jacket.' *Cornish Magazine*, Vol 1, p298,
    1898

Carew

Halliday, F.E., *A Cornish Chronicle*, Newton Abbot, 1967
Harris, Gladys and F.L. ed., *The Making of a Cornish Town*,
    Torpoint, 1976

Edgcumbe

Gill, Crispin, *Plymouth, A New History*. Exeter, 1993
Guides to Mount Edgcumbe, various

Eliot

Eliot, Robert. *Pocket Boroughs of the Eliot Family*.
    Journal, Royal Institution of Cornwall, 1985
Gill, Crispin, *Plymouth, A New History*. Exeter, 1993
Henderson, Charles, *Essays in Cornish History*, Oxford, 1935
Price, F.G.Hilton, *Handbook of London Bankers*, 1890-1
Reynolds, Royal Academy of Art Exhibition catalogue, 1986

Fox

Bradley, T.H., *The Fox Family of Falmouth*, Cornwall
    Association of Local Historians Magazine, Oct 1987
Davey, F.H., 'Penjerrick.' *Cornish Magazine*, vol II, p275, 1899
History of C.G.Fox & Co
Journals of Caroline Fox, ed Wendy Monk, 1973
Matthews, P.W. & Tuke, A.W., *History of Barclays Bank*, 1926
175 Years, 1772 to 1947. Anniversary letter from Fox Bros & Co
    Ltd, Wellington.
Whetter, James, *History of Falmouth*, 1981

Godolphin
Gill, Crispin. *Isles Of Scilly*, Newton Abbot, 1975
Smith, Marion, *Godolphin and its Owners*

Grenville
Gill, Crispin. *Buckland Abbey*, 1951
Rowse, A.L., *Sir Richard Grenville*, 1937

Killigrew
Bond, David, *Sir William Killigrew ...in Cornwall 1643-4. Cornish Studies* 1986
Graham, Winston, *The Grove of Eagles*, 1963
Henderson, Charles, *Essays on Cornish History*, Oxford 1935
Morley, Beric, *Castles of Pendennis and St Mawes*. English Heritage, 1988
Whetter, James, *History of Falmouth*, 1981
    The Thomas Killigrews, Old Cornwall, 1988

Molesworth-St Aubyn
Bailey, Caroline, *Rare Pleasures, Women and Home*, May 1990
Courtney, W.P., *Parliamentary Representation of Cornwall until 1832*, 1889.
MacLean, John, *Molesworth, Parochial and Family History of the Deanery of Trigg Minor*, 1873

Prideaux
Montgomery-Massingberd, Hugh. *Divine Inspiration*, Sunday Telegraph, 8 August 1887
Prideaux, R.M., *Prideaux, a Westcountry Clan*, 1990
Prideaux Place, *A guide*. 1990
Western Morning News , cuttings in library.

Rashleigh
Keast, John. *History of Fowey*, 1950

Agar-Robartes
Pearson, Jeremy, et al., *Lanhydrock, National Trust guide*, 1991

St Aubyn
Fletcher, Canon J.R., ed. by Dom John Stephan, *Short History of St Michael's Mount*, 1951
Pool, P.A.S, *William Borlase*, Truro 1986
St Aubyn, John, *St Michael's Mount*, 1974
Walling, R.A.J. *Story of Plymouth*, Plymouth, 1950

Treffry
Keast, John, *A Story of Fowey*, 2nd Edn 1983
Todd, A.C. & Laws, Peter, *Industrial Archaeology of Cornwall*, Newton Abbot, 1972
Thomas, D St J., *Regional History of Railways; The West Country*, 1960

Trelawny
Grylls, R. Glynn, *Trelawny*, 1950
Grigson, Geoffrey, *Freedom of the Parish*, 1954

Trevanion
Rowse, A.L., *The Byrons and Trevanions*, 1978

Vivians
Fielding, Daphne, *Mercury Presides*, 1954
    The Nearest Way Home, 1970
Mitchell, Dr P.D., Humphry Davy Lecture, Royal Institute of Cornwall, 1980
Obituary, 5th Lord Vivian, *Daily Telegraph*, 27 June 1991

Vyvyans
Lawrence, W.T., *Parliamentary Representation of Cornwall*, Truro
Vivian, Stanley, *The Story of the Vivians*, 1989
Vyvyan, C.C. *The Old Place*

Williams
Davidson, Robin. *Cornwall*, 1978.
Fitzmaurice, F.M., *A Chapter in Cornish Banking History*, Journal of the Royal Institution of Cornwall, 1991

Index